Before Roe

Before Roe

Abortion Policy in the States

Rosemary Nossiff

Temple University Press
PHILADELPHIA

Temple University Press, Philadelphia 19122
Copyright © 2001 by Temple University
All rights reserved
Published 2001
Printed in the United States of America

⊗ The paper used in this publication meets the requirements of the
American National Standard for Information Sciences—Permanence
of Paper for Printed Library Materials, ANSI Z39.48-1984.

Library of Congress Cataloging-in-Publication Data

Nossiff, Rosemary.
Before *Roe* : abortion policy in the states / Rosemary Nossiff.
    p.   cm.
  Includes bibliographical references and index.
  ISBN 1-56639-809-6 (cloth : alk. paper) — ISBN 1-56639-810-X
(pbk. : alk. paper)
    1. Abortion—Government policy—United States—States.
  2. Abortion—Government policy—New York (State).
  3. Abortion—Government policy—Pennsylvania.   I. Title.

HQ767.5.U5 N67 2000
363.46'09747–dc21   00-041194

For my mother,
  Mary Rose Sullivan Nossiff

Contents

Acknowledgments

In writing this book I drew on the support, commitment, and dedication of many people. Ted Lowi's enthusiasm and interest sustained me throughout. Another supporter was Elizabeth Sanders, who read the manuscript and offered several suggestions that improved it immeasurably. Martin Shefter's work and Benjamin Ginsberg's ideas about American politics influenced the way I approached this issue. My colleagues at Rutgers gave me a manageable teaching load that helped me to finish the book.

Scores of people generously agreed to be interviewed, giving me insights into this issue that were unavailable from secondary sources: Constance Cook, Lawrence Lader, Aryeh Neier, the Reverend Paul Gehris, Ruth Cusak, Lucinda Cisler, the Reverend Howard Moody, Thomas Noone, Howard Fetterhoff, Pat Miller, Dick Durand, Mary Winters, Jane Arnold, Ellen Willis, Marion Faux, and the women at CHOICE, People Concerned for the Unborn Child, and the Committee for Progressive Legislation. Their commitment to this issue deepened mine. I would also like to thank the unnamed activists on both sides of the debate who enhanced this analysis and helped me reach an understanding of its numerous dimensions.

Special thanks to Glen Halva-Neubauer, whose research on post-*Roe* abortion politics in Pennsylvania enriched mine, and who generously gave me the names of various people who helped me in different ways. One of these was Morgan Plant, whose political connections helped me locate the people and information I needed across the state, and whose hospitality made my trips to Harrisburg more enjoyable. I am also grateful to Doris Braendel for her suggestions on how to revise the original manuscript. All these people contributed to this book, but any errors of interpretation or fact are mine alone.

Julie Copenhagen and the rest of the reference staff at Olin Library at Cornell University provided me with outstanding assistance, regardless of the request, from start to finish. My thanks to the Schlesinger Library at Radcliffe Institute, Harvard University, for permission to quote from its Family Planning Oral History Project Records. I also wish to thank Claudia Morner at the Dimond Library at the University of New Hampshire, who extended full privileges to me during the summers while I was working on the book, and to the law firm of Burns, Bryant, Hinchey, Cox, and Rockefeller for the use of their library.

My thanks to Stacey Young, Tim Byrnes, and Martha Jurchak for their e-mails, advice, phone calls, and visits, and to Martha Raimon and Nancy Ries for reading chapters of the manuscript as well. My sisters Christine and Virginia, my brother Joe, and my cousin Ness were invaluable as I struggled to come to terms with my mother's death, which occurred while I was putting the manuscript together. This book is for her.

Finally I thank my husband, Michael Scammell, whose dedication to this book was second only to mine. From reading chapters and commenting on the manuscript to making dinner three nights a week, his support and commitment never wavered, and for that I am deeply grateful.

Before *Roe*

Introduction

Few issues in contemporary American politics have remained on the public agenda as long or split the country as divisively as abortion policy. Its inherent political, social, and moral dimensions make it an explosive issue that no institution, group, or religion has succeeded in containing.

It was not always so. Until the nineteenth century it was not difficult for most women to have an abortion into the fifth month of pregnancy, generally with no penalty. It was only in the 1850s that the American Medical Association sponsored an antiabortion campaign in a bid to professionalize medical practice. By 1900, the AMA had succeeded in passing laws that made abortions illegal, except when the woman's life was endangered, in almost every state and territory. These laws remained in force until the 1960s, when groups across the country employed a combination of legislative, judicial, and political campaigns to change them. The result was the 1973 landmark decision in *Roe v. Wade*, in which the Supreme Court held that laws prohibiting elective first-trimester abortions were unconstitutional because they violated women's right to privacy.[1]

The seeds of the controversy were sown in the seven years immediately preceding *Roe*. It was then, when the legislatures and the courts attempted to reconcile religious opposition to abortion with individuals' civil liberties, that the battle lines were drawn. The struggle began with the 1965 Supreme Court decision in *Griswold v. Connecticut*, which identified a right to privacy that protected married

1

couples' access to contraceptives.[2] Using *Griswold*, pro-abortion activists on the state level argued that women's access to abortions in certain circumstances was similarly protected, and they began campaigns to change the laws.

In the pre-*Roe* period between 1965 and 1972, thirteen states liberalized their statutes to allow abortions when the woman's health was endangered, and in cases of rape, incest, and fetal deformity. Four, including New York, repealed their abortion laws. One, Pennsylvania, tightened its law to make abortions more difficult to obtain. The remaining states retained their laws prohibiting all abortions except when the woman's life was in danger.[3] These conflicting policies provided fertile ground for forces on both sides to further their causes in the courts and legislatures, pitting women's right to privacy against states' rights to regulate abortion and protect maternal and fetal health.

Oddly enough, few books have comparatively examined the pre-*Roe* period, which is central to understanding the roots of the conflict.[4] There are several ways to examine pre-*Roe* abortion policy: an analysis of all fifty states, a comparison of the thirteen reform states, a case study of a single repeal state. Each has its limitations. An aggregate approach on the national level would identify some of the reasons that abortion bills were passed in certain states and not in others by examining such factors as religious demographics and the number of interest groups involved. But it could not provide the kind of microanalysis needed to describe the interaction between the Catholic Conferences, political parties, and interest groups on the state or local level. These factors, which significantly shaped pre-*Roe* politics, would probably be identified by an in-depth case study, but critics of this approach question the applicability of one state's findings to another. Given the political profile of each state, how can a consensus be reached on which factors are most important in shaping abortion policy?

To avoid these pitfalls, this book compares pre-*Roe* abortion politics in New York with those in Pennsylvania, the two states that led the nation in creating abortion policy both before and after *Roe*. Although an argument can be made that early reform states such as California (1967) and Georgia (1968) were the forerunners in creating pre-*Roe* policy, the laws that they and eleven other states passed essentially legalized a widespread medical practice and affected only a tiny number of women whose pregnancies met the strict guidelines discussed above.

New York and Pennsylvania were the first states in this period to pass legislation that went beyond reform, albeit in different ways. In 1970 New York passed the least restrictive abortion bill in the country, allowing abortions in the first and second trimesters of pregnancy, with few restrictions. Two years later, neighboring Pennsylvania tightened its law to prohibit all abortions, except when the woman's life was endangered. Although this law was vetoed by Governor Shapp, in 1974 Pennsylvania passed the first of four abortion control acts and became a leading state in the pro-life movement. New York, whose 1970 statute the Supreme Court used in crafting *Roe,* remains one of the fourteen states that funds Medicaid abortions.[5]

Although no claim is made here that what happened in New York and Pennsylvania explains pre-*Roe* abortion policy in its entirety, these two cases provide rich insights into how party systems on the state level dealt with abortion policy before *Roe*, the role that grassroots and interest groups played in placing it on the political agenda, and how the nature of the discourses employed by various forces altered the parameters of the debate. In addition, the two states' positions, at opposite ends of the policy continuum, necessitate an examination that accounts for the entire range of pre-*Roe* abortion policy. To broaden this approach, case studies of other pre-*Roe* abortion states are included here.[6]

Divergent Neighbors

In the 1960s, New York and Pennsylvania shared several political characteristics that make them particularly well suited for comparative purposes. Both were large, industrial states with major metropolitan areas containing racially diverse populations. Mayhew (1986) classifies them as "regular organization states" with traditional party structures, partisan elections, and machine politics.[7] Both New York and Pennsylvania exhibited urban-rural cleavages, with the Democratic party dominating the cities, and the Republican party thriving in rural areas.

In terms of religious demographics, Catholics made up 36% of New York's population in 1970 and 31% of Pennsylvania's. With regard to the Jewish population, there was a significant difference between the states. In New York Jews comprised 11.8% of the population, compared to 4.0% in Pennsylvania. Since Jews constitute a potent political force in New York politics, and hold a generally secular view of abortion that defines access to abortion as a civil right, they provided a strong counter to Catholic influence on the abortion question in New York.

However, more important than demographics is how religious groups are politically mobilized. In a study of abortion rates on the state level since *Roe*, Hansen (1980) found that the measure of Catholic influence, rather than the absolute number of Catholics in a given state, offers a better explanation for the differences in the number of abortion providers and abortion rates.[8] Similarly, in their analysis of pre-*Roe* abortion laws, Mooney and Lee (1995) concluded that the probability of a state reforming its abortion laws was negatively associated with the percentage of Catholics and fundamentalist Protestants in the population.[9] My research supports these findings and shows that before 1973, the influence that Jews in New York had on abortion policy was more a result of the open party system in the 1960s than of their numbers.[10]

When pre-*Roe* abortion bills were introduced, both states had governors who were pro-abortion, and both had well-established Catholic Conferences.[11] Public-opinion polls in New York in 1968 and in Pennsylvania in 1972—along with nationwide polls—showed majority support for abortion reform for physical or mental health reasons, yet neither state's policy reflected these preferences.[12] Given these similarities, one might have expected their abortion policies to have resembled those passed in the other states before *Roe,* or at least to have resembled each other. In fact, they could scarcely have been more different. The question is why.

This book attempts to solve this policy riddle by examining how political developments in the 1950s shaped the opportunities for abortion activism in the 1960s, the nature of the responses by the political parties, and the way abortion forces and grassroots groups institutionalized their respective discourses in the legislatures and the courts. In other words, it tries to understand how opportunities, parties, groups, and discourse interacted to create abortion policy before *Roe,* using the insights of institutional and political-opportunity theory. Blending these theoretical perspectives provides a fuller and more accurate analysis than either can supply alone, and builds upon the areas where they overlap.

This analysis rests on the view of recent institutionalists that political and institutional changes are conditioned by the historical period or "political order" within which they occur, a pattern similar to that which social-movement theorists refer to as "cycles of protest."[13] Reform matters. The abortion campaigns in New York and Pennsylvania appeared in the wake of a national reform movement that occurred in various machine-dominated cites after World War II. Although these movements were concentrated in Manhattan and Philadelphia, the dissimilar approaches taken by the reformers, discussed in Chapter One, affected the Democratic Party in New York and Pennsylvania in different ways, and influenced the kinds of abortion policies each state adopted.[14]

Since efforts to change the abortion laws in all states were aimed first at the legislatures and later at the courts, an examination of institutional developments in the 1960s is essential to an understanding of the pre-*Roe* period. Rules have great significance, both for what gets accomplished and for what doesn't. They shape the efforts of political actors by reconciling their interests with broader purposes. Arguably, rules govern the legislative process in favor of institutional goals as opposed to democratic ideals of representation—although not always, as we will see. They regulate access to the floor and allow dominant forces to contain public debate, as was demonstrated by the successful efforts of the Catholic Conferences in New York and Pennsylvania in the mid-1960s to kill abortion bills in committee, before they reached the floor.

By the pre-*Roe* period, the rules governing standing in the courts had been expanded. This development was a particular boon to pro-abortion activists, whose lack of financial resources was mitigated by the free legal representation offered by attorneys and others interested in civil-rights litigation. The relative swiftness with which the courts heard abortion cases in the seven-year period between the decisions in *Griswold* and *Roe* can also be accounted for by the number of "movement suits"[15] brought by feminists, which challenged restrictive abortion laws.

In the debate over abortion policy, the key struggle in the past two centuries has been over this question: What is being aborted, an embryo, a fetus, or a child? Whose rights are given priority? As E. E. Schattschneider noted, "The definition of the alternatives is the supreme instrument of power. . . ."[16] Thirty years later, Maarten Hajer observed that "The study of discourse opens new possibilities to study the political process as *mobilization of bias.*"[17] Schattschneider's paradigm of power, in which competing forces attempt to narrow or widen the scope of the conflict for political leverage, supports the interpretation of discourse as a political weapon that groups use first to shape the way in which policy issues are understood, second to discredit their opponents, and third to bring about change. There are two ways to do this. One is in the legislatures; the other is through the courts.[18]

The centrality of discourse and framing to the abortion debate is discussed in Chapter Two, which traces the medical, religious, and legal discourses employed by activists on both sides. The key role played by feminist discourses in shaping the legal and political arguments used to repeal the abortion laws, and also in mobilizing activists and creating communications networks, is analyzed in Chapter Three. Although several states reformed their laws in the 1960s, the *repeal* of abortion laws took place only after the women's movement had emerged.[19]

Mediating between institutions and the public are political parties. As agents of the parties, legislators and governors attempt to reconcile interest groups' demands and electoral realities within the restraints imposed by institutional structures. The case studies of New York and Pennsylvania in Chapters Four and Five show why the degree of party support proved crucial to the success of early abortion campaigns. In New York, pro-abortion activists were aligned with the reform element of the Democratic Party, which helped them get annual abortion-reform bills introduced and, beginning in 1966, brought them into the policy stream. In Pennsylvania, antiabortion forces were able to block reform with the help of the Democratic leadership, which was aligned with the Pennsylvania Catholic Conference on reproductive issues.[20]

The taboo surrounding abortion delayed the formation and limited the effectiveness of most groups concerned with abortion policy until around 1970. With the exception of the National Conference of Catholic Bishops and its administrative arm, the United States Catholic Conference, none of the main interest groups involved, including the Clergy Consultation Service, the National Organization for Women, and the National Association for the Repeal of Abortion Laws, was an established player.[21] For this reason an accurate analysis of the pre-*Roe* era must include the actions of individual abortion activists and grassroots groups, as well as those of legislators and interest groups.

Chapter Six analyzes the effect of public discourse by contrasting the strategies of the successful forces in each state with those of their opponents. A chief reason for the victories of the pro-abortion activists in New York and the antiabortion forces in Pennsylvania was that they selected framing strategies in accord with the political opportunities they encountered; the New York activists, in fact, changed their approach when it became politically advantageous.

The unsuccessful activists in each state disregarded political developments for different reasons, and in Pennsylvania they forged ahead with a strategy that backfired.

Chapter Six also shows, however, that without the structural changes to the party system effected by reform campaigns in New York and Pennsylvania, neither the use of particular framing strategies, nor the participation of groups, nor the availability of resources adequately accounts for the policy discrepancies between the two states. Therefore, the analysis that follows examines partisan and institutional developments as well as the discourses and resources used by groups to show why New York and Pennsylvania passed vastly different pre-*Roe* policies.

Roe ignited rather than extinguished the debate over abortion by asserting that the states had an interest in protecting potential life prior to viability. For the next fifteen years, the courts, rather than the legislatures, were the key institutions making abortion policy. The *Roe* decision and its aftermath are assessed in Chapter Seven, with an analysis of the pro-life movement in Pennsylvania, one of the movement's flagship states.[22]

The legislative developments in Harrisburg provide a particularly apt context to measure pro-life activists' success in crafting restrictive abortion policy within the confines established by *Roe*. In 1989 a new Supreme Court revisited *Roe*, and in its five-to-four decision in *Webster v. Reproductive Health Services*, it returned to the states some of the power they had lost in 1973.[23] By 1990, twenty-five years after *Griswold*, the struggle had been renewed on the state level, where it had begun.

Without question, people's positions on abortion are shaped by a myriad of social, moral, and economic factors. But ultimately abortion policy is decided in the political arena. This book examines how one of the most intimate decisions a woman makes, whether to continue or terminate a pregnancy, has become one of the most politicized issues in contemporary American politics.

Notes

1. *Roe v. Wade*, 410 U.S. 113 (1973).

2. In *Griswold v. Connecticut*, the Court held that a Connecticut law that prohibited the sale of contraceptives to married couples was unconstitutional because it violated the individual's right to be left alone, as guaranteed by the First, Fourth, Fifth, and Ninth Amendments (381 U.S. 471 [1965]).

3. In addition to the four repeal states—Hawaii, New York, Alaska, and Washington—the District of Columbia allowed early abortions for any reason. In Mississippi a woman's life had to be endangered, or she had to be the victim of rape, to obtain a legal abortion. In New Hampshire and Louisiana abortions were technically prohibited because their statutes did not include therapeutic exceptions. In Pennsylvania the statute prohibited illegal abortions but did not define the difference between legal and illegal ones. See Chapter Five. For a list of pre-*Roe* abortion laws in the state, see Craig and O'Brien 1993, p. 75. See also Tatalovich and Daynes 1981, p. 24.

4. Although most books on abortion include a brief summary of the pre-*Roe* period, only two provide a detailed discussion of the events before 1973. Lawrence Lader's *Abortion II: Making The Revolution* (1973) is predominantly a study of the antiabortion movement before 1973. The author provides a detailed overview of the New York campaign and examines the political developments that led to the formation of the National Association for the Repeal of Abortion Laws, of which he was a founder. Much of the basic information contained in Chapter Four comes from Lader's account. Tatalovich and Daynes's *The Politics of Abortion: A Study of Community Conflict in Public Policymaking* (1981) analyzes the agenda-setting process of abortion politics between 1960 and 1980. Their focus is primarily on the policy-making process, and they examine the effect of public opinion and organized interests on abortion policy.

5. During the pre-*Roe* period, those in favor of reforming or repealing the abortion laws were referred to as "pro-abortion"; those opposed to changes were "antiabortion." After 1973 these names were replaced by "pro-choice" and "pro-life," for reasons discussed in Chapter Seven.

6. There are six single-state pre-*Roe* case studies: Jain and Gooch, *Georgia Abortion Act 1968* (1972); Jain and Hughes, *California Abortion Act* (1969); Jain and Sinding, *North Carolina Abortion Act* (1968); Steinhoff and Diamond, *Abortion Politics: The Hawaii Experience* (1977); Kristen Luker's *Abortion & the Politics of Motherhood (*1984), which examines pre-*Roe* abortion politics in California to analyze the worldviews of activists on both sides of the debate; and Marion Faux's account of the Texas challenge, *Roe v. Wade: The Untold Story of the Landmark Supreme Court Decision That Made Abortion Legal* (1988).

7. Mayhew 1986.

8. Hansen 1980, p. 385.

9. Mooney and Lee 1995, p. 619.

10. Ebaugh and Haney (1980) found that for the period between 1972 and 1978, Jews had more liberal attitudes on abortion than did Protestants or Catholics. This interpretation of the Jewish view of abortion was voiced by Rabbi Balfour Brickner, an early member of the Clergy Consultation Service. Interview with Brickner, March 24, 1998, New York, N.Y.

11. Strictly speaking, the first abortion-reform bill was introduced in Pennsylvania in 1967 (SB 38) when Governor Raymond Shafer, who opposed abortion reform, was in office. This bill was part of a broader effort to update the Pennsylvania Constitution as opposed to being a reform bill per se. Aside from SB 38, which died in committee, all the pre-*Roe* abortion bills were introduced when Milton Shapp, an abortion-reform supporter, was governor. Nelson Rockefeller, who favored reform, was governor of New York throughout the pre-*Roe* period.

12. Beginning in 1965, public-opinion polls showed majority support for abortions in cases of rape, incest, fetal deformity, and danger to the mother, yet only eighteen states in this period reformed or repealed their laws (Tatalovich and Daynes 1981, p. 118). On New York, see Lader 1973, p. 122. On Pennsylvania, see Walsh 1974, p. 4.

13. For an overview of recent approaches to the study of political change, see Dodd and Jillson 1994, especially Orren and Skowronek on political order. On cycles of protests, see Tarrow 1994.

14. My discussion of reform politics focuses on the Democratic Party in New York and Pennsylvania because in both states it was the party most active in pre-*Roe* abortion politics. The Republican Party in New York was instrumental in passing the 1970 abortion repeal law, but its involvement came in the last stages of the battle. The bill's passage was more the result of Constance Cook's feminism than of her party affiliation, though her party standing undoubtedly helped the repealers. Although the Republican machine had dominated politics in Pennsylvania from the

Civil War to the 1940s, the GOP in Pennsylvania did not become a player in abortion policy until the post-*Roe* period, as was the case for the GOP nationwide.

15. These suits also were brought in an effort to raise public awareness and shape the public discourse about illegal abortions. See Rubin 1987, pp. 49–50.

16. Schattschneider 1960, p. 68.

17. Hajer 1993, p. 45.

18. Activists on both sides also used public opinion, but as a means to an end. On the process of discourse institutionalization, see ibid., p. 46.

19. Exactly when any social movement begins is debatable, but the 1970 Women's Strike For Equality seems a logical starting point, in that it was the first national demonstration of the women's liberation movement.

20. I use the term "activists" to describe challengers and "forces" to describe groups seeking to maintain the status quo, with slight variation depending on context.

21. The one exception was the American Civil Liberties Union, whose members worked on pre-*Roe* abortion cases.

22. The reasons for and significance of the change in the terms used to describe antiabortion activists after 1973 is discussed in Chapter Seven.

23. *Webster v. Reproductive Health Services*, 492 U.S. 490 (1989).

1 Reform and Opportunity

When pro-abortion activists in New York and Pennsylvania began their campaigns to change the abortion laws, the obstacles they faced were similar: public opposition to reform, well-organized opponents, party indifference, and limited resources. Yet within five years the state legislatures in Albany and Harrisburg had passed radically different policies. Why activists in New York triumphed while their counterparts in Pennsylvania were defeated can be traced to a number of interdependent factors.

The most important factor was the progress of political reform, because it affected both the degree of access new forces had to the parties and the political opportunities and resources available. The varying degrees of openness encountered by pro-abortion activists in New York and Pennsylvania in the 1960s had a significant impact on the abortion policies passed in each state before *Roe*. This, in turn, affected the kinds and amounts of resources available to them and their ability to challenge dominant forces.

Reform Politics

The movement for political reform in America emerged in the wake of the Civil War, and subsided roughly 100 years later with the gradual demise of the political machines. The

13

reform ideal united Mugwumps, Populists, and Progressives in the belief that political participation should be motivated by personal commitment and civic virtue, as opposed to political favors promised by the party bosses. Generally speaking, reformers charged their opponents with varying degrees of corruption and inefficiency. Outnumbered by immigrants whose political allegiance was to the boss, they traditionally capitalized on elite dissatisfaction with party government and on internal factions within the parties to build support to challenge the machine.

The national reform movement that emerged during the Progressive Era at the turn of the century laid the foundation for a series of reform campaigns in party-machine states, including New York and Pennsylvania, that continued for the next fifty years. The most successful political reform effort in nineteenth-century Philadelphia was begun in the 1870s by the Quakers, who formed the Committee of One Hundred to expose the corruption of the public gas utility.[1] In 1894 the National Municipal League, the first national reform organization in the country, was established in Philadelphia by delegates to the First Annual Conference for Good City Government.[2] This was followed by several unsuccessful attempts to change Philadelphia's city charter, beginning in 1901 and ending in 1939. The backbone of all these campaigns were various civic organizations.

This "blue-ribbon" approach to reform reflected Philadelphia's Quaker traditions and its British heritage.[3] The Quaker attitude to conflict, where consensus is favored over compromise, encouraged participation through civic organizations as opposed to political parties. This attitude was shared by the British upper class, which generally disdained politics as a vocation. In both cases, private philanthropy

was the preferred method of elites to solve social problems—
a preference reinforced by the Philadelphia reformers' lack
of electoral success in changing the city charter.

Throughout the late nineteenth century, civic elites in
New York attempted to topple the Democratic Party's infa-
mous machine, Tammany Hall. Unlike their counterparts
in Philadelphia, however, the Manhattan reformers aligned
with Republicans and other anti-Tammany forces, and in
1901 they formed a fusion coalition that intermittently succeeded in electing three reform mayors, most notably
Fiorello La Guardia in 1933.[4] After twelve years of his
administration, Tammany Hall no longer had the ability to
channel all political activity in the city,[5] and the seeds of the
contemporary party-reform movement had been sown.

After World War Two, both cities weathered reform
movements, but the developments described above shaped
their forms and outcomes. In Philadelphia a new breed of
reformers emerged with political aspirations based on a New
Deal philosophy of government as a positive social force.[6]
Led by Richardson Dilworth and Joseph Clark, upper-mid-
dle-class attorneys with political ambitions, a "good government" coalition consisting of civic groups, the business
community, and social-science professionals gave birth in
1949 to the "Philadelphia Renaissance," a decadelong
municipal-reform campaign aimed at putting the city's
affairs in order. In Manhattan the "reform" Democrats, who
represented the interests of constituencies at odds with the
machine, competed for control of the Democratic Party with
the "regular" Democrats, whose ties remained to the organization.[7] The different outcomes of the reform movements
in New York and Philadelphia in the 1950s affected how
open the party system in each state was to abortion-policy
changes in the following decade.

Philadelphia Reform

The modern history of reform in Pennsylvania began in the late 1940s with the unsuccessful campaign of Richardson Dilworth for mayor of Philadelphia. Revelations of municipal graft and corruption formed the basis of Dilworth's campaign against the Republicans in the 1947 Philadelphia race. Throughout his campaign, Dilworth leveled specific attacks against incumbent Republicans, accusing them of being associated with organized crime.[8] Although the Republicans denounced Dilworth in the press, he had already established a large personal following, which became his future campaign base. After his defeat in the election, he was elected chairman of the Americans for Democratic Action, a group of professionals and activists interested in political careers. The ADA later became a campaign vehicle for Dilworth and to a lesser degree Joe Clark.[9]

Mayor Bernard Samuel, the Republican who defeated Dilworth, realized how much political support the idea of municipal reform had attracted in the campaign. Shortly after his victory he appointed The Committee of 15, a group of local citizens, to suggest ways to improve the city's efficiency. The following year, an investigation into the city's finances revealed well-entrenched practices of graft and corruption in several city departments.[10] This led to more investigative reports, and was followed by the suicide of four city officials including an employee of the Amusement Tax Office, who left a note that accused tax-office employees of embezzling public funds.[11]

Another significant result of the committee's findings was its recommendation of the adoption of a new city charter, which contained a home-rule provision for Philadelphia.[12] The adoption of the city charter became the campaign platform of the ADA.[13] It was also the catalyst for a group of prominent city leaders to organize The Greater Philadelphia Movement, aimed at insuring the ratification of the new charter. Although the GPM drew people from education and labor, control of the group rested with business leaders, who had concluded that corruption in the city was threatening the business community. The GPM's involvement was characteristic of past efforts in Philadelphia, where elites had pursued reforms through a proposed new city charter.

With support for reform growing, it became clear that the Democrats could sweep city hall.[14] In the off-year election in 1949, the Democrats drafted Richardson Dilworth to run for city treasurer, and his former campaign manager, Joe Clark, for city controller.[15] As a result of the scandals and Dilworth's name recognition, the Democrats won the 1949 election by 100,000 votes.[16]

After taking office, Clark and Dilworth cooperated with the Democratic organization by employing party supporters.[17] In return, in 1951 the Democrats nominated Clark to run for mayor, and nominated Dilworth, who had lost races for mayor and governor, for district attorney. This strategy was highly successful, with Clark and Dilworth carrying every district in the city except those in the Republican stronghold known as the River Districts.[18] In addition to voting in a reform administration, city voters ratified the Home Rule Charter.

Once secure in their new positions, however, Clark and Dilworth distanced themselves from the Democratic Party in order to reform city government. Instead of giving city jobs to party regulars, Mayor Clark used civil-service examinations to fill city positions and hired outside experts as well.[19] He upheld the newly ratified charter, which further weakened party power, and he strictly enforced several of its provisions, including barring city employees from engaging in political activity and requiring proof of incompetence before a city employee could be dismissed, thus protecting the jobs of competent employees who happened to be Republicans.[20]

Clark and Dilworth were municipal as opposed to party reformers; they were primarily concerned with the mismanagement of the city, not with reforming the party. They underestimated the machine's organizational strength on the precinct level and its ability to deliver votes, and they did not attempt to gain control of the party apparatus or create a third party to weaken it. An address made by Dilworth to the American Institute of Planners in 1957 shows his lack of concern with party politics. "When you think about it," he said, "our reform movement was sparkplugged by the planners not the politicians! The first impetus to move the city out of the rut came from those concerned about corruption, and the push for a city seen in terms of organized planning brought about the demand for orderly and honest government. This is probably a unique experience."[21] Although it was characteristic of elite reformers,[22] Clark and Dilworth's underestimation of the party was also due to their political inexperience and the state of the Democratic Party after decades of Republican control in Philadelphia. The mutual dependence of the reformers and machine Democrats to keep the Republicans out of power, along with the regulars' fear that the reformers had more public support than the party did, enabled Clark to secure the party's nomination, if not its blessing.[23] In 1956 Clark was elected to the U.S. Senate, with Dilworth succeeding him as mayor.

By the time Dilworth ran for governor in 1962, however, the regulars had regained the upper hand. Their gradual comeback had begun in 1953 with a newly mobilized

Democratic machine consisting of disgruntled Democratic regulars and crossover Republicans. The election of two Democratic governors, George Leader in 1954 and David Lawrence in 1958, further signaled the regulars' increasing strength. Unable to overpower the Democratic city chairman, William Green, Leader turned over thousands of patronage jobs to the machine.[24] Lawrence, as Democratic state boss, had funneled patronage to the Democratic machines in Philadelphia and Pittsburgh since the New Deal, and continued to do so in the 1960s.[25]

During the 1962 gubernatorial race between William Scranton and Dilworth, Scranton exploited the reformers' weak hold on the party by tarring them with the regulars' brush: "I think the Republicans have an awfully good issue here on this bossism business which doesn't please me in the least."[26] Scranton beat Dilworth by half a million votes. One key factor that contributed to Dilworth's 1962 defeat was his attempt while mayor of Philadelphia to cooperate with the machine and amend the city charter so that a person could hold more than one political office at a time.[27] It failed, and Dilworth was forced to resign in the middle of his second term. This botched attempt also helped the organization reassert itself by casting doubt on the altruism of the reformers. The underhanded manner in which Dilworth attempted to amend the charter, the so-called "secret agreement" he made with the Democratic organization soon after his election as mayor, cost him support from Democratic reformers and reform-minded Republicans in his run for governor.[28] In a neat twist, Scranton successfully incorporated the reform theme created by Dilworth into the campaign against him.

Despite Governor Scranton's campaign promises to rid the state of "bossism," both the Democratic organization and the Republican machines remained powerful.[29] In the early 1960s the regular Democrats recaptured Philadelphia with the mayoral elections of Raymond Tate in 1963 and 1967 and Frank Rizzo in 1971. Within fifteen years of their triumph over the machine, the reformers' ascendancy had ended, and a political climate hostile to challengers, including the pro-abortion activists, had returned.[30]

The New York Reformers

Beginning in the late 1950s, reform forces in Manhattan launched a campaign to gain control of the Democratic Party. New York's postwar regime of New Deal liberals and Democratic machine politicians faced the usual charges of corruption and financial mismanagement, and came under attack for other reasons as well.[31] New York City's population was decreasing and changing: Established populations of older residents, including groups of Italians and Irish, were being replaced by middle-class professionals in lower Manhattan, and by blacks and Puerto Ricans in Harlem.[32] These demographic changes yielded a constituency for young attorneys and social workers, who disagreed with the city's treatment of the poor and racial minorities, and for journalists who objected to the omnipotence of the public-works czar, Robert Moses.[33]

Another wing of the postwar reform forces in New York included people politicized by Adlai Stevenson's 1950s presidential campaigns. "We would never have grown up without Adlai Stevenson," stated, the executive director of the New York Committee for Democratic Voters. "He, so far as I'm concerned, is the spiritual and intellectual leader of the reform movement."[34] Finally, business interests, which were disenchanted with the city's fiscal policies, and Republicans, who considered party reform to be one way to increase their limited influence in the city, joined the reform coalition to demobilize the machine.[35]

The reformers launched a three-pronged campaign aimed at Tammany Hall, Robert Moses, and various social-service agencies in the city.[36] By broadening their attack, they succeeded in attracting support from a range of disaffected groups and in effecting a split between the reform Democrats and the "regular" Democrats, who were struggling to retain control of the party organization and city offices. By the early 1960s, the reform Democrats had begun to oust the regulars by capturing the leadership of various assembly districts in Manhattan.[37] In 1965 the reform coalition triumphed over the machine with the election of a fusion mayor, John Lindsay.

The Manhattan reformers resembled their Philadelphia counterparts in terms of education and class, but there were two significant differences that shaped the abortion policies that the states passed before *Roe*. The first was the inclusion of women. Previous reform clubs in both states had excluded women, but the Manhattan reformers included both married couples and single women. Women in the reform clubs were often employed outside the home, and were more likely to be interested in and supportive of abortion reform than were homemakers, who were more identified with child-raising.[38] As Irene Davall, an early member of the Chelsea Democratic Club, put it, "If it hadn't been for us, [abortion reform] wouldn't have come up."[39]

The second difference was the New York reformers' strategy of controlling city politics by taking over the party from within, as opposed to changing the city charter.[40] The chief advantage of this approach was that it provided the reformers with an established infrastructure that helped them institutionalize their agenda and build new constituencies. They were also able to make use of the political clubs in each assembly district, which formed a loose communications network throughout the city. The reformers' control of these clubs later proved critical to the success of pro-abortion activists in New York. Beginning in 1965, the clubs sponsored forums and debates on abortion policy. These events legitimized the issue and allowed the activists to reach thousands of potential supporters. The club members' political experience and their ability to effect changes within the party made them especially valuable.

In New York, the struggle within the Democratic Party enabled pro-abortion activists to align with the reformers, who needed their support to gain control of the party from the regulars. This resulted in annual abortion-reform bills being introduced—the first step in gaining access to the political process. In Pennsylvania, the return of the Democratic machine in the early 1960s sharply limited the access of new groups such as the pro-abortion activists, and delayed the annual introduction of abortion bills there until 1970.

Political Opportunity

The different types of reform campaigns in New York and Pennsylvania meant that the party systems and political opportunities that groups on both sides of the debate encountered were radically different in the two states. Most theories of political opportunity, though they vary to some degree, concentrate on the ability of established groups and forces to control access to the political system and to shape policy.[41] As Tarrow points out, the most salient dimension

of opportunity structure is the stability of political alignments.[42]

Herbert Kitschelt's analysis of the antinuclear movements
in four countries provides a useful way to asses systemic permeability.[43] Kitschelt found that a nation's political opportunity structure—"specific configurations of resources, institutional arrangements, and historical precedents"—shapes
the receptivity of a political system to challengers, and influ-
ences policy outcome.[44] The closed nature of Pennsylvania's
party system helped the Pennsylvania Catholic Conference
(PCC) rebuff the attempts of pro-abortion activists to change
the laws. In New York, the intraparty struggle between regular and reform Democrats resulted in a system that was
more open to new constituencies.

Differences in opportunity structures and resources,
however, cannot alone account for policy discrepancies.
Aggrieved groups must act, and part of the decision to mobilize has to do with their perception of their chances of success. Mario Diani's research on the Northern League provides insights about framing processes that can be applied to
the strategies employed during the pre-*Roe* debate. Like
Kitschelt, Diani examined the stability of political alignments, but he also cross-classified it with actors' perceptions
of opportunities for autonomous action, and he identified
the framing strategies that were most likely to achieve policy success for challengers.[45] When applied to the case studies of New York and Pennsylvania, Diani's topology shows
why the framing strategy used by pro-abortion activists in
Albany succeeded in articulating new policy demands and
why it backfired in Harrisburg and played into the hands of
the PCC.

Another central component of challengers' perceptions
of their chances concerns their consciousness. In their

analyses of poor people's movements, Piven and Cloward (1977) describe three stages: (1) Leaders and the institutions they run lose legitimacy among generally law-abiding citizens, who (2) begin to assert their rights and (3) believe they can change existing arrangements.[46] Similarly, McAdam considers "cognitive liberation" an essential element of generating movement insurgency.[47] Freeman's analysis of the early days of the women's-liberation movement identifies "a climate of expectations that something would be done" as part of the foundation supporting the movement.[48]

Once the opportunities and the perceptions of success develop, challengers need resources. Social-movement theorists disagree on what kinds of resources are needed to fuel insurgency. Some assign more importance to elite participation and consider resources such as money, political contacts, and the support of professionals to be critical to a movement's emergence. Others argue that such resources as leaders within the community, communication networks, and consciousness-raising discourses are more important in mobilizing supporters.[49]

Staggenborg has shown that in the pre-*Roe* period, pro-abortion activists relied on a combination of elite and grassroots resources. This was true of the successful forces in New York and Pennsylvania as well. In Albany, early legislative and interest group support were critical to the later success of pro-abortion activists. But so, too, was the participation of radical feminists in Manhattan and upstate women's church groups, who united to create electoral support for repeal throughout the state. In Harrisburg, the PCC's legislative support for restrictive abortion policy was greatly enhanced by the statewide grassroots campaigns against abortion that emerged in the late 1960s. In contrast, the unsuccessful forces in New York and Pennsylvania failed to attract this mix of elite and grassroots backing, which significantly narrowed their bases of support and decreased their ability to shape the outcome.

By any measure, the resources of the Catholic Church in the 1960s dwarfed those of their opponents. But the one domain where pro-abortion activists could effectively challenge the Church was the public discourse. It is for this reason that defining abortion became the focal point of the pre-*Roe* debate.

Notes

1. For a history of the influence of the Quakers and civic organizations in Pennsylvania reform politics, see Petshek 1973, pp. 8–9]. See also Crumlish 1959.

2. Judd 1988, p. 85.

3. Petshek 1973, Ch. 1.

4. These were Seth Low in 1901, John Purroy Mitchell in 1913, and Fiorello La Guardia in 1933. See Lowi 1963, Ch. 8.

5. Shefter 1985, pp. 34–35.

6. Petshek 1973, p. 56.

7. This distinction between reform and regular Democrats is similar to the one between amateur and organization men made by Wilson 1962, pp. 2–3. Of course, what constitutes "reform" is an open question; here it means a change from the status quo.

8. The following discussion is based on Freedman 1963 and Reichley 1959. Parts of this section also appear in my article (1995).

9. Leon Shull, director of the ADA in Pennsylvania from 1951 to 1964), telephone interview, January 11, 1993.

10. Freedman 1963, p. 22.

11. Ibid. and Petshek 1973, p. 27.

12. Crumlish 1959, p. 18.

13. The ADA's platform included the following: (1) city-county consolidation, (2) the repeal of legislation that discouraged the creation of a fusion party, (3) city council elections free of party identification, (4) the elimination of straight party voting by machine, and (5) stronger regulations concerning merit system employment (ibid., p. 23]).

14. Ibid. and Reichly 1959, p. 11.

15. Ibid. p. 12.

16. Freedman 1963, p. 23.

17. Reichly 1959, pp. 12–13.

18. Freedman 1963, p. 24.

19. Reichly 1959, p. 16.

20. Freedman 1963, p. 25.

21. Quoted in Petshek 1973, p. 17.

22. Banfield and Wilson (1963, p. 144) note that blue-ribbon reformers cannot try to gain control of the party without losing the support of elites.

23. Petshek 1973, p. 68.

24. Ibid.; Keiser 1990, p. 51.

25. On Lawrence, see Weber 1988. On machine politics in Pittsburgh, see Stave 1970.

26. Quoted in Beers 1980, p. 293.

27. Although Clark crossed the machine regarding the city charter and civil service, he sought its support on other issues and, in exchange for party backing of his fiscal policies, agreed not to raise taxes (Banfield 1965, pp. 110–11).

28. Leon Shull interview. See also Petshek 1973, pp. 69–70.

29. Scranton's main reform effort was in the area of civil service, where he protected half of the state's public-service positions (Beers 1980, pp. 297–98).

30. Although the reformers decreased the machine's power, as seen in the narrowing margins by which organization candidates beat their opponents, the regulars nonetheless succeeded in electing their candidates for mayor of Philadelphia from 1963 to 1978. For a different interpretation of the reform movement's contribution to Philadelphia politics, see Keiser 1990, Ch. 3 and Petshek 1973, Ch. 12.

31. The following discussion of reform politics in New York is based extensively on Shefter 1985, especially Ch. 3, 4, and 5, and Wilson 1966, Ch. 2.

32. Wilson 1996, pp. 41–42.

33. Shefter 1985, pp. 46 and 49.

34. Quoted in Wilson 1966, p. 52.

35. Shefter 1985, pp. 62 and 75.

36. Ibid., p. 42.

37. Wilson 1966, p. 35.

38. This distinction between traditional and less traditional women supports the profiles of activists involved in the campaign for the equal-

rights amendment and the abortion movement. See Mansbridge 1986 and Luker 1984.

39. Davall, who later joined the National Organization for Women, wrote letters to reform clubs in the city, speaking at some and asking others to support abortion reform. Interview with Irene Davall, November 21, 1997, New York, N.Y.

40. Wilson 1966, p. 40.

41. On the general concept of political opportunity see Eisinger 1973, Tilly 1978, McAdam 1982, Kitschelt 1986, and Tarrow 1994. In connection with the women's movement, see Freeman 1975, Staggenborg 1991, and Costain 1992.

42. Tarrow 1994, p. 86.

43. Kitschelt 1986, p. 62. Both Tarrow's identification of the four dimensions of political opportunity structure (p. 86) and Kitschelt's discussion of the openness of political regimes to new demands (p. 64) are concerned with what Tarrow terms the stability of political alignments. Here, cleavages between elites increase challengers' access to parties and institutions, and to policy coalitions. The distinction between open and closed systems is also discussed by Eisinger.

44. Kitschelt 1986, p. 58.

45. These are realignment, inclusion, antisystem, and revitalization (Diani 1996). See Chapter Six for a discussion of how these frames were used in New York and Pennsylvania in the pre-*Roe* period.

46. Piven and Cloward 1977, pp. 4–5.

47. McAdam 1982, p. 48.

48. Freeman 1975, p. 52.

49. Resource-mobilization theorists generally stress the importance of elite resources, whereas their opponents concentrate on the importance of resources that are indigenous to activists. For a good discussion of the differences between them, see Ch. 2 of McAdam 1982. On the women's movement, see Freeman 1975 and Ch. 1 in Staggenborg 1991.

2 Competing Discourses

Why a topic becomes a political issue is a central question addressed by theorists of agenda-setting.[1] Although these theorists focus on different aspects of the agenda-making process, what unites them is the significance they assign to discourse as a tool used by competing forces to get their respective issues into the policy stream. Discourse is the critical link between grievance and action. As Edelman notes, "political beliefs, perceptions, and expectations are overwhelmingly not based upon observation or empirical evidence available to participants, but rather upon cuings among groups of people who jointly create the meanings they will read into current and anticipated events."[2] These cuings are often based on the discourses introduced by political actors who seek to control policy outcomes. For example, until the nineteenth century, when physicians defined abortion as murder, most people did not consider early abortion to be a criminal offense. Similarly, it was not until radical feminists in the 1960s defined access to abortion as central to women's liberty that people made that connection.

To make sense of the conflicting discourses provided by competing forces in any policy debate, people order ideas and concepts around narrative structures or stories that resonate with their beliefs and principles.[3] The concept of discourse coalitions, "a group of actors who share a social construct" and act on it, describes the process by which various groups of people who view an issue in a similar way form coalitions and organizations and attempt to shape policy outcomes.[4] This approach to policy analysis highlights the significance of discourse in agenda-setting by focusing on the "story lines" or narratives that unite coalitions, and that shape their definitions of problems and the solutions they propose.[5] The concept of discourse coalitions is particularly relevant to the pre-*Roe* debate, where different story lines united opposing sides. Antiabortion forces adopted a narrative based on the sanctity of human life to build support against abortion reform; pro-abortion activists argued that restrictive abortion laws violated women's rights to privacy, equality, and liberty, and were therefore unconstitutional. Antiabortion groups favored prohibiting access to abortions; their opponents proposed reforming and later repealing the existing abortion laws.

Discourse coalitions frame an issue in a particular way, promoting one set of values over another—in this case the sanctity of human life versus the right to privacy. This is an especially significant dimension of the abortion debate, given the inherent ethical nature of the issue. The elasticity of discourse coalitions, which enables them to unite various groups with related but somewhat different views on an issue, was well suited to the abortion conflict because differences soon emerged within each coalition in terms of how strict or loose the laws should be.[6]

On the antiabortion side, some individuals and organizations were prepared to allow abortions when the embryo was likely to be severely deformed, while others thought that no exceptions should be made, except when the woman's life was endangered. The factions were united, however, in their opposition to the vast majority of abortions and their support of legislation to make abortions more difficult to obtain. Within the pro-abortion coalition, some members favored allowing abortions in cases of crimes, deformity, or when the pregnant woman's health was endangered, while others held that all abortion restrictions should be repealed. Generally speaking, however, they all agreed that existing abortion laws should be made less restrictive.

The focal point of the conflict over abortion policy was thus how to define abortion. Since the nineteenth century, various groups had argued that their respective positions qualified them to regulate abortion policy. Physicians framed abortion as a medical issue and maintained that their expertise, their duty to care for all stages of life, and their role in determining when a woman's life was threatened by a pregnancy gave them a deciding voice on the issue. Attorneys argued that since abortion regulations conflicted with fundamental rights, the courts were the arena in which abortion policy should be created. The Catholic Church regarded abortion as a predominantly moral and religious issue, which it considered itself best suited to define and regulate. In the late 1960s, radical feminists claimed that access to abortion was a central component of women's liberty, and that the decision to have an abortion should be made by the woman involved, not by her doctor, the Church, or the State.[7] From conservative Catholics to radical feminists, all these actors attempted to control abortion policy by promoting specific discourses to define the issue, and by framing their policy demands in a way that spoke to their broader political goals.

The professional, legal, and political discourses analyzed in this chapter are characteristic of the frameworks that are often used to define a broad range of social-policy issues.[8] Just as discourses are not neutral, neither are the frameworks within which they are embedded. Professional frameworks stress expertise; legal frameworks follow established rules or define issues in terms of conflicting rights; political frameworks assume that a compromise between interested parties or ideological foes will best resolve the issue.[9]

These frameworks generally serve the interests of their respective supporters, and sometimes, though not always, they coincide with the public good. Abortion policy can be categorized by more than one framework at a time, allowing groups such as physicians and members of the clergy, or civil-rights advocates and feminists, to align with each other even if their goals are not identical. In the pre-*Roe* period, competition among groups and the frames they advanced led to the formation of two main discourse coalitions. The pro-abortion coalition consisted of physicians, lawyers, civil-rights activists, public-health officials, and feminists, and they challenged existing abortion laws with a combination of discourses that favored either reforming or repealing the laws. Most members of the antiabortion coalition before 1973 were affiliated with the Catholic Church, which used its political arm, the U.S. Catholic Conference, and its state affiliates to propagate a religious discourse advocating the retention of restrictive abortion laws on the state level.

Professional Framing

Between 1800 and 1900, abortions were widely performed,[10] and the practice of abortion before quickening[11] was not considered to be a criminal offense under common law. By the mid-1840s abortion was commonplace, and it probably would have remained so had it not been for the establishment of the American Medical Association in 1847.[12]

Like many other associations founded in the nineteenth century, the AMA was organized to promote professional standards, which varied considerably throughout the country. Ten years after its founding, Dr. Horatio Robinson Storer began a campaign through the AMA's societies on the state level to change public opinion about abortion, and to lobby legislatures to pass laws outlawing its practice.[13] The following quote, from a doctor's speech at a local medical society meeting in 1873, expresses the spirit of the physicians' campaign against abortion: "Many, indeed, argue that the practice is not, in fact, criminal, because, they argue, that the child is not viable until the seventh month of gestation, hence, there is no destruction of life. The truly professional man's morals, however, are not of that easy caste, because he sees in the germ the probable embryo, in the embryo the rudimentary foetus, and in that, the seven months viable child and prospective living, moving, breathing, man or woman, as the case may be."[14]

Why many physicians supported restrictive abortion laws can be traced to a variety of moral, medical, and economic reasons.[15] Some doctors active in the antiabortion campaign believed that life was sacred. Others questioned the morality of abortion by citing the Hippocratic Oath, which was interpreted by some to forbid abortions; trained physicians considered adherence to the oath the dividing line between themselves and nonmedical practitioners—primarily midwives.[16] The quickening standard, as a reliable scientific basis for determining the beginning of fetal life, was also questioned by some doctors.

Although some doctors supported restrictive abortion legislation for altruistic reasons, others became active in the campaign against abortion chiefly to restrict midwives, their main competitors, from providing health care to women. As Wertz writes, "Doctors worried that, if midwives were allowed to deliver the upper classes, women would turn to them for treatment of other illnesses and male doctors would lose half their clientele. . . ."[17] Nativist concerns also prompted some physicians to oppose abortion.[18]

One reason for the success of the physicians' antiabortion campaign was the absence of opposing groups. Although the nineteenth-century women's movement was organized by the 1860s, the majority of feminists were primarily concerned with securing the vote for women. Like the antiabortion physicians, many of them considered abortions to be a degrading procedure that exploited women, and they supported the AMA's attempts to criminalize it.[19] They also argued, however, that the reason so many women had abortions was their husbands' uncontrolled sexual drives, not their own moral ineptitude: "Till men learn to check their sensualism, and leave their wives free to choose their periods of maternity, let us hear no more invectives against women for the destruction of prospective unwelcome children, whose dispositions, made miserable by unhappy antenatal conditions, would only make their lives a curse to themselves and others."[20]

The solution proposed by the feminists reflected their sensibilities: the education and enfranchisement of women.[21] In any event, feminists opposed abortion because they viewed the necessity for it as an indication of the sexual exploitation of women by men, rather than as a means to women's equality.[22]

In essence, the AMA's antiabortion campaign propagated a moral and medical definition of when life began, within the broader framework of professionalism. This duality satisfied both the moral concerns of doctors, by stating that the embryo was a life, and their medical concerns, by declaring that only physicians were properly trained to perform abortions in cases where the woman's life was threatened.

An activist in Michigan expressed it like this: "It is not sufficient that the medical profession should set up a standard of morality for themselves, but the people are to be *educated up* to it. The profession must become aggressive towards those wrongs and errors which *it only* can properly expose, and successfully oppose."[23]

The timing of the physicians' campaign coincided with the wave of professionalization in public policy that followed the Civil War. Doctors' improving status enabled them to press for restrictive abortion laws, especially during Reconstruction, when legislators believed that expertise was crucial to the formation of the new administrative state.[24] By defining abortion as a moral and medical issue, and articulating their demands in ways that served legislators' broader goals, the physicians gained control of a widespread practice, increasing their professional power and providing a pretext for asserting their claims of scientific primacy over midwives and other nonmedical competitors. By 1900, the physicians had succeeded in criminalizing all abortions, except when the woman's life was endangered.

The AMA's control over abortion remained unchallenged until the 1950s, despite medical advances that decreased the need for abortions in cases of chronic illness, such as heart disease and diabetes. A study released in 1951, however, showed that a surprisingly high number of therapeutic abortions were still being performed by physicians, though most of the reasons they gave did not, strictly speaking, constitute legal grounds for the procedure.[25]

This situation eventually led to a split within the medical profession. On one side were "strict constructionists," who argued that abortions should be performed only when the woman's life was endangered; on the other were "broad constructionists," who also took into consideration

the woman's mental health, the likelihood of fetal deformity, and the emotional health of the family.[26] So successful was the medical community in asserting its claims of
expertise that it was not until the late 1950s, when doctors
became divided over the issue of therapeutic abortions and
concern grew over the legal implications of performing
them, that other professionals joined the debate over abortion policy.

In 1957 Planned Parenthood, which had been organized
by birth-control activists in the early 1940s, held a conference to discuss the advisability of reforming laws to legalize
therapeutic abortions. The conference passed a resolution
requesting that the American Law Institute (ALI) and the
Council of State Governments conduct studies to create a
model law that could be used to update state laws on abortion.[27] Two years later, the ALI drafted the following model
penal code, which defined justifiable abortions: "A licensed
physician is justified in terminating a pregnancy if he
believes that there is substantial risk that continuance of
the pregnancy would gravely impair the physical or mental
health of the mother or that the child would be born with
grave physical or mental defect, or the pregnancy resulted
from rape, incest, or other felonious intercourse."[28]

For physicians who supported a strict constructionist
view of abortion, the ALI guidelines, while broadening the
definition of justifiable abortions, nevertheless bolstered
their position by affirming that abortion fell within their
area of expertise.[29] For those favoring a broader definition,
the guidelines let them make the case that abortion policy
was an issue of doctors' rights. Overall, the ALI definition of
abortion provided the medical profession with a rights
framework that enhanced its control of abortion policy and
protected physicians from prosecution by the State.

In the early 1960s, two related events brought the idea of abortion-law reform home to the average person. The first was the case of Sherri Finkbine, hostess of the children's television show *Romper Room*, who discovered that a tranquilizer she took while pregnant contained thalidomide, a drug linked to fetal deformity. To warn other women, she told her story to a newspaper reporter. As a result, the public hospital that was to have performed her abortion refused to do the procedure.[30] Finkbine, who traveled to Sweden to have an abortion, later wrote about her decision:

> I am not a doctor who can give you medical insights into the
> dangers of illegal abortion, nor a lawyer who can speak on
> the absurdities of our archaic laws. I am not a religious person
> with dogma decrying the murderous aspects of the subject.
> I am a person who is much more deeply involved than any
> of those people could ever be. I am a mother who desperately
> needed a pregnancy terminated. I can truthfully say to you
> that an abortion was to me a very sad, ugly experience, but
> definitely the lesser of two evils.[31]

Two years after the Finkbine episode, there was an outbreak of rubella, a disease linked to fetal deformity if contracted by a pregnant woman.[32] These incidents heightened awareness of abortion by raising questions about abortion policy. Was it ethical to deny an abortion to a woman whose fetus was likely to be severely deformed? Should women victims of rape or incest be required to carry a pregnancy to term? Was it fair that women with money were generally able to obtain abortions through medical contacts while most poorer women were not?

These concerns, together with the ALI guidelines, merged into an abortion-reform discourse that supported the legalization of therapeutic abortions. The strength of the ALI reform discourse was twofold: It articulated a growing concern among both health-care professionals and the public about illegal abortions, and it presented a solution to a newly recognized problem that was supported by elites and the public. After the Sherri Finkbine episode in 1962, Gallup asked a national sample the following question: "As you may have heard or read, an Arizona woman recently had a legal abortion in Switzerland after having taken the drug thalidomide, which has been linked to birth defects. Do you think this woman did the right thing or the wrong thing in having this abortion operation?"[33] Slight majorities (52 percent) in all groups except Catholics thought Finkbine had done the right thing.[34] Public opinion polls between 1965 and 1972 indicated support for reform.[35] A 1965 poll conducted by the National Opinion Research Center showed majority support for abortions in "hard" cases—where the woman's life was endangered (73 percent), in cases of fetal deformity (57 percent), and in cases of rape (59 percent). "Soft" cases were a different matter: The approval rate was only 18 percent when the reason for the abortion was that the woman was unmarried, 16 percent when she was married but did not want any more children, and 22 percent when the family income was low. Still, the high numbers in the "hard" cases showed that support for some change in the laws did exist, and it was in this climate of public opinion that pro-abortion activists began their campaign to reform the law.

Legal Framing

Griswold v. Connecticut

The 1965 decision in *Griswold v. Connecticut* marked the beginning of the legal debate over abortion. The case was brought by Estelle Griswold and Charles Lee Buxton, who opened a clinic in New Haven in 1961 to provide birth-control counseling and to distribute contraceptives. As they expected, they were arrested soon after the clinic opened. They were convicted, and they appealed their conviction through the Connecticut courts up to the U.S. Supreme Court.

The legal discourse informing the debate over abortion policy in the 1960s was based on a "positive theory of privacy," which the Supreme Court had created a decade earlier.[36] The foundation of this new theory was the concept of "zones of privacy," areas that the State was constitutionally prohibited from regulating.[37] This approach contrasted with the Court's narrower interpretation of the Fourth and Fifth Amendments in the first half of the century, when evidence of physical trespass or unintentional self-incrimination was necessary before an individual could claim that her privacy had been threatened.[38]

The path toward *Griswold* can be found in the dissenting opinions of the Supreme Court in the 1961 case *Poe v. Ullman*,[39] in which the plaintiffs were seeking declaratory judgments on Connecticut statutes that prohibited the use of contraceptive devices and the giving of medical advice concerning their use. The Court determined that the cases in question did not meet its standard of controversy and therefore dismissed the claims, but in his dissent, Justice John M. Harlan argued in favor of using due process to invalidate Connecticut's laws. "It is not the particular enumeration of rights in the first eight Amendments which spells out the reach of Fourteenth Amendment due process," Harlan wrote, "but rather, as was suggested in another context long before the adoption of that Amendment, those concepts which are considered to embrace those rights which are . . .

fundamental; which belong . . . to the citizens of all free governments."[40]

Also in dissent, Justice William O. Douglas provided the argument that the majority later used in *Griswold:* "When the State makes 'use' a crime and applies Criminal sanction to man and wife, the State has entered the innermost sanctum of the home. If it can make this law, it can enforce it. And proof of its violation necessarily involves an inquiry into the relations between husband and wife. That is an invasion of the privacy that is implicit in a free society. . . . This notion of privacy is not drawn from the blue. It emanates from the totality of the constitutional scheme under which we live."[41]

Four years later, writing the opinion for the Court in *Griswold v. Connecticut,* Douglas reiterated his definition of birth control as a private matter that the State could not regulate: "The present case, then, concerns a relationship lying within the zone of privacy created by several fundamental constitutional guarantees. And it concerns a law which, in forbidding the use of contraceptives rather than regulating their manufacture or sale, seeks to achieve its goals by means having a maximum destructive impact upon that relationship. Such a law cannot stand in light of the familiar principle, so often applied by this Court, that a 'governmental purpose to control or prevent activities constitutionally subject to state regulation may not be achieved by means which sweep unnecessarily broadly and thereby invade the area of protected freedoms.' "[42]

The value of *Griswold* to the pre-*Roe* abortion campaign was initially noted by Thomas Emerson in a 1965 law-review article on the legal aftermath of *Griswold.* Emerson observed that by using the Ninth Amendment as the basis of the decision, the Supreme Court had provided constitutional grounding for an unspecified but recurrent right to privacy, and opened the way "for an attack upon significant aspects of the abortion laws."[43]

Two years later, an article by Roy Lucas developed the legal significance of Emerson's thesis and laid out the grounds for a judicial challenge: "Moreover, present abortion laws are (1) largely unenforced, (2) uncertain in scope, (3) at odds with accepted medical standards, (4) discriminatory in effect, and (5) based upon the imposition by criminal sanction of subjective religious values of questionable social merit upon persons who do not subscribe to those values."[44]

For abortion activists, the significance of *Griswold* was threefold. First, it created a "zone of privacy" in marital areas, including birth control, with which the state could not interfere, and it established the right to privacy as part of the constitutional guarantees of the Bill of Rights and the Fourteenth Amendment. As Rubin has noted, "The importance of *Griswold* was that it picked up and articulated a widespread concern for privacy, gave it a constitutional grounding, and tied it to precedent and traditional political theory. For the first time, the Court acknowledged that such a right, implicit in our tradition of individualism and limited government, was basic enough to our society to be given constitutional dimensions."[45]

Second, by invalidating state laws prohibiting access to contraceptives, *Griswold* legitimized their use by married couples, thus shaping the public discourse on the issue of birth control. Third, by grounding the concept of privacy in the Bill of Rights and the Fourteenth Amendment, the decision provided a precedent for future civil-rights litigation.[46]

Since the early 1960s, activists in California had been organizing to liberalize the state's abortion law. Initially,

Griswold's main effect was to induce other states to join the campaign. In New York, pro-abortion activists used it as the basis of their legislative and judicial campaign.[47] *Griswold* situated the debate over abortion policy precisely because the case specifically addressed birth control. Although most activists and organizations involved in the campaign to change the abortion laws did not consider abortion to be a routine method of birth control on a level with contraceptives, it was, nonetheless, a way to end a pregnancy in extreme cases. The ruling enabled pro-abortion forces to make the argument that if access to contraception was part of marital privacy and was protected from State interference, abortion should be included on those grounds as well.[48]

Reform Laws

Between 1966 and 1972, thirteen states enacted ALI-type abortion statutes. Although the laws varied, they all permitted therapeutic abortions under certain circumstances.[49] The reform position suited the majority of early pro-abortion activists, who were accustomed to working with legislators and interest groups. It allowed them to use the kinds of insider resources they had, such as professional and personal contacts, to generate support for incremental change.[50] Given the controversial nature of the abortion issue in the mid-1960s, a more direct and confrontational approach probably would have backfired.

The importance of framing abortion reform within terms they could control was evident early on to abortion activists across the country, although the discourses they employed varied. In California, where reform bills had been introduced as early as 1961, pro-abortion activists used a medical discourse to build broad-based support for abortion reform.

In 1966, the California State Board of Medical Examiners charged several prominent physicians with performing illegal abortions, though all the abortions had been for pregnant women exposed to rubella. As a result, thousands of physicians who had been previously inactive joined the reform campaign. One activist described the process:

> This is the way it worked. A small group of distinguished physicians drafted and revised and finalized a statement on abortion and the problems of illegal abortion; it said why the law constituted a barrier to good health care, was inequitable and illegal and unconstitutional, and was ill advised and dangerous and shocking for a civilized society. And then that statement, with the names of the initial signers, was sent to a large number of physicians in the state. [Similar statements were sent to] lawyers, ministers, social workers, and sociologists. I guess there were four statements in all, and there were thousands of signatures.[51]

Pro-abortion forces in California used the Catholic Church's antagonism to their advantage by arguing that those opposed to reform were religiously motivated, a charge that delegitimized antiabortion forces in the eyes of some members of the medical community.[52]

In North Carolina, which in 1967 became the second state in the country to pass an abortion law based on the ALI guidelines, pro-abortion activists framed the debate in predominantly legal terms.[53] They did this because a medical discourse would have played into the hands of the many attorneys in the legislature who enjoyed "putting doctors in their place."[54] In addition, the activists considered a legal discourse an effective way to discourage the participation of groups concerned with population growth and birth control, issues that might have generated controversy. Since the Catholic proportion of the population in North Carolina was the smallest in the nation in 1966 and was not a politically

powerful constituency, pro-abortion supporters characterized opposition to the bill as "a Catholic issue," and the
Church probably realized that a vigorous campaign against
reform would be futile.

In Georgia, where a reform bill was passed in 1968, pro-
abortion forces used a medical discourse that stressed the
technical rather than the moral dimensions of the issue.
Unlike in North Carolina, where supporters judged that a
medical discourse would antagonize legislators who were
also attorneys, pro-abortion activists in Georgia framed
abortion reform as way to protect physicians, who had
more public support than lawyers.[55] By steering clear of the
moral aspects of the bill, pro-abortion forces preempted the
active participation of Catholic Church, whose influence
in Georgia was stronger than its small numbers would
suggest.[56]

An initial advantage of the reform discourse was that it
enabled pro-abortion forces to avoid the kind of conflict that
would have been created by a feminist discourse, which
framed access to abortion as a woman's right.[57] Despite the
early success of reform forces in several states, however, it
soon became evident that the ALI laws were inadequate to
stem the tide of illegal abortions because the laws affected
only a small minority of women—those whose pregnancies
were the result of a crime or posed health problems. Another
weakness of the reform position was its ambiguity, for the
reform arguments shifted with the circumstances: For some,
abortion was acceptable when the woman's life was endangered, but not in cases of fetal deformity; others felt that
abortion was acceptable in both instances. These factors
splintered support for reform and promoted divisions within
the pro-abortion coalition.

By the late 1960s, the legal premise underlying the ALI
laws—that abortion was primarily a physicians'-rights

issue—was becoming problematic for the more radical elements within the coalition. Although activists were encouraged by the passage of ALI laws in several states, the limited scope of the laws induced some to press for abortion repeal. By 1969 the discourse on abortion policy had moved from moderate demands for reform to a radical demand for repeal. Writing in that year, former Supreme Court Justice Thomas Clark summarized the Court's rulings on the relationship between liberty and family life, and crystallized the issue for the Court.

> The result of these decisions is the evolution of the concept that there is a certain zone of privacy which is protected by the Constitution. Unless the State has a compelling subordinating interest that outweighs the individual rights of human beings, it may not interfere with a person's marriage, home, children, and day-to-day living habits. This is one of the most fundamental concepts that the Founding Fathers had in mind when they drafted the Constitution. No one will deny that a State has a valid interest in regulating the well-being of its inhabitants, especially when it is dealing with children, who are more susceptible to undesirable influences. We have also seen that a State may not unreasonably interfere with the intimate relations of its inhabitants. When deciding on the constitutional constraints imposed on a State's interference with individual rights, the vital question becomes one of balancing. . . . I submit that until the time of life is present, the State could not interfere with the interruption of pregnancy through abortion performed in a hospital or under appropriate clinical conditions. I say this because State interference is permissible only if reasonably necessary to the effectuation of a legitimate and compelling State interest. Prior to that time that life is present in the fetus, what interest does the State have?[58]

Political Framing

Religious Groups

Although the Catholic Church and some Protestant churches opposed abortion in the nineteenth century, neither religion joined the physicians' campaign to criminalize it.[59] In 1869, Pope Pius IX declared that all abortions, regardless of the age of the fetus or the medical reasons involved, were grounds for excommunication, because of the Church's belief that the soul exists from conception.[60] But given the small percent of Catholics in the country and anti-Catholic sentiment at the time, it's likely that the Church felt that its involvement in legislative politics would be counterproductive, perhaps even dangerous.[61]

The Protestant Churches, the largest religious institution in the country, had a different problem. Since most people did not believe that the fetus was a human life before quickening, Protestant ministers would have had considerable difficulty convincing their parishioners that abortion was wrong. For these reasons, both churches were content to let the physicians take the lead.[62] It is true, however, that the Catholic Church's support of the Comstock laws in the nineteenth century, and its opposition to birth control, laid the ground for its later opposition to abortion reform.[63]

The Catholic Church established its contemporary position on abortion policy only in 1965, with the conclusion of Vatican II, a series of meetings concerning the role of the Catholic Church in contemporary society. One of the main resolutions of Vatican II was to bring the Church into the modern world by involving it in current social and religious problems. The Church's commitment was soon tested by the Johnson Administration's plans to include federally funded birth control programs as part of the War on Poverty.[64] Some conservatives opposed the programs and urged the Church to do the same.[65] While the Church was grappling with problem, the issue of abortion reform was also emerging. Although abortion policy had not yet become a political issue, it was defined in the Pastoral Constitution, one of the documents written during Vatican II: "For God, the Lord of Life, has conferred on men the surpassing ministry of safeguarding life—a ministry which must be fulfilled in a manner worthy of man. Therefore, from the moment of its conception, life must be guarded with the greatest of care, while abortion and infanticide are unspeakable crimes."[66]

By encouraging the Church to become involved in a wider range of issues, Vatican II indirectly increased the authority of the bishops.[67] As Byrnes writes, "Given Catholic teaching on abortion and the bishops' mission to relate that teaching to the world beyond the church, one can hardly imagine a policy initiative more likely to capture the attention and galvanize the efforts of the American hierarchy in the mid-1960s than the liberalization of abortion laws."[68]

In 1966, a year after Vatican II concluded, the Catholic hierarchy reorganized the conference, which had represented the Church in Washington since World War I, and replaced it with two organizations. The National Conference of Catholic Bishops (NCCB) was established to unify and strengthen the bishops' political voice; the United States Catholic Conference (USCC) was created to administer its programs.[69] A new director was appointed to lead the Family Life Bureau of the USCC, Monsignor James McHugh, and beginning in the fall of 1966 the bureau sponsored a national symposium on marriage and held a series of regional meetings of Family Life Directors.[70]

Also in 1966, the bureau aligned itself with the National Right-to-Life Committee to coordinate the increasing number of local antiabortion campaigns. From the start, the committee's strength was on the grassroots level, and the Division urged the dioceses to form local units in each state. The relationship between the Church and the committee was a symbiotic one: by allowing non-Catholics to join, the Church was able to challenge its opponents' charges that opposition to abortion was solely a Catholic issue.[71] Meanwhile, the Church's administrative support and membership base helped the committee expand its fledgling campaign against abortion reform.

In 1967, the NCCB included $50,000 in its budget to oppose abortion reform on the state level.[72] As bills to make therapeutic abortions legal began passing in several states, the USCC responded by stepping up its opposition. In April of 1967 it held a national meeting of the Family Life Directors to improve communications between them and the dioceses. It sent information on proposed changes in abortion legislation to Catholic Conferences on the state level, and held several regional meetings to organize support against abortion reform.[73] In June of 1967, the USCC sent a memo to the bishops, advising them of its plans to monitor the growing debate over abortion policy:

> In keeping with the directive of the Administrative Board, the USCC Family Life Bureau has been serving as a communication center and coordination agency in regard to the general trend around the country to change the abortion laws. We foresee this effort continuing through the next three to five years, and in this time we will continue to formulate materials and provide communications among the dioceses and state conferences. . . . Because the continuing efforts to change the laws must be confronted on the state level, it is most important that our Bureau maintain communications with some designated person or persons in each diocese. We will be to able to supply information pieces and a continual overview as to what

happens in other sections of the country. At the same time, the contact person will be able to keep us up to date on the campaign in his state and provide you with the latest information.[74]

The attempts to change abortion laws on the state level presented the Church with a moral and institutional dilemma.[75] As noted earlier, the Church considered all forms of artificial birth control (as opposed to natural approaches, such as the rhythm method) to be immoral because they were seen to interfere with one of the main purposes of married life: procreation.[76] Abortion was a graver matter both theologically and morally, because the Church viewed it as the destruction of human life. Institutionally, the Church suspected that if abortion-reform efforts succeeded, the result would be the withdrawal of public funds from Catholic hospitals unwilling to perform abortions.[77]

One way out of this dilemma was proposed by Robert Drinan, a leading Catholic theorist and dean of the Boston College law school. Writing in 1967, Drinan suggested that if Catholics joined the majority of the public who favored legalizing abortion in cases where the woman's life was endangered, they would have more success in mobilizing public opinion to prevent abortions in cases of rape, incest, and fetal deformity, and where the pregnancy was not wanted or could not be afforded.[78] Although the Catholic hierarchy ignored Drinan, this strategy was successfully employed by the other main religious group active during the pre-*Roe* period, the Clergy Consultation Service on Abortion.[79]

The CCS was the brainchild of an abortion activist named Lawrence Lader. Lader contacted the Reverend Howard Moody, the Baptist minister of the Judson Memorial Church in Manhattan, about involving the clergy in the pro-abortion campaign.[80] Moody held a series of meetings with other religious leaders in the city to discuss what kind of role the clergy might play in providing referrals for therapeutic abortions.[81] By deciding to help women obtain therapeutic abortions, the CCS established the type of negotiating dialogue characteristic of political frameworks, where interests are required to compromise to resolve policy disputes. The CCS forced the hand of the Catholic Conference, rhetorically speaking, by articulating a competing religious position that invited pro-reform people of various faiths to join the debate. The ecumenical nature of the clergy participating in the CCS further increased its influence.

In 1967, in its first public statement on the issue, the CCS challenged the Catholic Church's central assertion that life begins at conception, and supported physicians who performed therapeutic abortions: "We affirm that there is a period during gestation when, although there may be an embryo life in the fetus, there is no living child upon whom the crime of murder can be committed. When a doctor performs such an abortion motivated by compassion and concern for the patient, and not simply monetary gain, we do not regard him as a criminal but as living by the highest standards of religion and of the Hippocratic Oath."[82]

The establishment of the CCS was a turning point in the reform campaign because it was the first organization to publicly provide abortion referrals, and, in the words of Howard Moody, "to free that word up. To free it from silence, from the whispered things. People need to be able to things."[83] The CCS was also the catalyst that led several other religious denominations to establish their positions on abortion, including the Unitarian Universalists, who endorsed abortion reform in 1963, and the Episcopal Church. Both groups became active in the New York reform campaign.[84] Except for the groups mentioned above and a scattering of individual churches and synagogues on the state and local levels, no other major religions became actively involved in supporting abortion reform before *Roe*.

By the end of 1968, the medical, legal, and political/religious discourses around abortion reform had been established. Activist physicians, attorneys, clergy members, and various individuals interested in issues of public health and birth control were jockeying to regulate abortion policy on the state level, where five states had passed ALI laws.[85] Although these coalitions differed in their approaches to abortion reform, each viewing the problem from its area of expertise, none of them viewed the issue within the framework of sexual identity. It was at this point that another group joined the effort and altered the terms of the debate irrevocably.

Notes

1. Cobb and Elder (1972) analyze the importance of "triggering events" in increasing the salience of a given issue, which, in turn, increases initiators' access to the agenda. Baumgartner and Jones (1993) examine the dynamic that occurs when the "policy image"—the beliefs and values characterizing an issue—combines with the biases of the particular venue that challengers select to institutionalize their demands, which can range from an agency of the federal government to a municipal court. The degree of success actors achieve in effecting desired policy changes depends partly on their ability to identify the most hospitable institution. Snow, Rochford, Worden, and Benford (1986) focus on the process of framing, or "the use of ambiguity and multiple interlocking themes to construct a simple, singular square that limits and controls the meaning of some significant object or event," as a central component of political participation and policy implementation. On the concept of the policy stream, see John Kingdon 1984. Parts of this chapter appear in my article "Discourse, Party, and Policy" (1998).

2. Edelman 1971, p. 32. On the relationship between cues and collective action, see also McAdam 1982.

3. Stone 1989, p. 282. See also Luker's analysis of the connection between worldview and abortion (1984, Ch. 7).

4. Hajer 1993, p. 45.

5. Stone 1989.

6. Hajer 1995, p. 65. Hajer applies this term in describing the two competing groups attempting to shape acid-rain policy in Britain and the Netherlands.

7. The abortion discourse created by radical feminists in the 1960s is discussed in Chapter Three.

8. In addition to these categories, Kirp includes two others: bureaucratic or administrative regulations, and market forces, both of which became more significant after the *Roe* decision. For a general discussion of the five frameworks, see Kirp 1982. See also Diesling 1962.

9. Kirp 1982 pp. 138–39. The Catholic Church falls into the political framework in this analysis, as its actions against abortion in the pre-*Roe* period were predominantly in the political arena. Unlike other political actors, however, it rejected any compromise on abortion policy, due to the religious dictates governing it.

10. For a discussion of social and economic factors that affected the practice of abortion in nineteenth-century America, see Petchesky 1984, pp. 73–74.

11. The term "quickening" refers to the time when a woman can feel the presence of the fetus, which is generally in the fourth or fifth month of pregnancy.

12. The first efforts to regulate abortions came in the 1820s, when several state legislatures passed statutes addressing abortion practices. These laws were part of wider efforts to revise criminal codes and to control attempted murder by poison (many abortifacients of the time were poisons) rather than direct attempts to regulate abortion (Mohr 1978, pp. 20–22). This discussion of the nineteenth-century abortion movement is based extensively on Mohr.

13. Mohr 1978, p. 148.

14. Ibid. pp. 165–66.

15. See ibid., pp. 35–37, 165–67.

16. Ibid., p. 35.

17. See Wertz and Wertz 1989, p. 55.

18. Mohr 1978, p. 166.

19. See ibid., Ch. 4. See also Petchesky 1984, Ch. 1.

20. Quoted in ibid., p. 112.

21. Ibid.

22. This argument continues to inform pro-life activists. See, for example, Luker (1984, Ch. 7) and Ginsburg (1989, Ch. 9). Pro-life activists I interviewed also felt that easy access to abortion "let men off the hook."

23. Mohr 1978, p. 171.

24. Ibid. p. 203.

25. Therapeutic abortions refer to those performed in cases of rape, incest, or fetal deformity, or when the woman's physical or mental life is endangered. See Russell 1951, pp. 435–36. Russell also compared the incidence of therapeutic abortions in several hospitals in different periods and showed similar ratios. See also Gebhard et al. 1958, Rosen 1954, and Williams 1957.

26. This distinction between physicians is made by Luker 1984, pp. 76–80.

27. Francome 1984, p. 102.

28. Schambelan 1992, pp. 82–83.

29. Luker p. 72.

30. Ibid. p. 64. Finkbine flew to Sweden and obtained a therapeutic abortion there.

31. Finkbine 1967, p. 15.

32. Ibid. p. 80.

33. Quoted in Tatalovich and Daynes 1981, p. 116.

34. Forty-nine percent of Catholics disagreed with Finkbine's decision, with thirty-three percent in agreement (ibid.).

35. *Public Opinion*, May/June 1989, p. 34.

36. Westin 1967, p. 350. For a discussion of this period, see Chapter Thirteen.

37. Ibid. p. 353.

38. Ibid. pp. 340–43.

39. *Poe v. Ullman*, 367 U.S. 497 (1961).

40. *Poe v. Ullman* at 541.

41. *Poe v. Ullman* at 520–21.

42. *Griswold v. Connecticut* at 485.

43. Emerson 1965.

44. Lucas 1968, p. 752.

45. Rubin 1982, p. 40.

46. Faux 1988, p. 75.

47. Lader 1973, p. 12.

48. For further discussion of the effect *Griswold* had on pro-abortion strategy, see ibid., p. 12; Faux 1988, p. 77; and Sarvis and Rodman 1974, p. 95.

49. For a list of the variations among states that reformed their abortion laws in the pre-*Roe* period, see Craig and O'Brien 1993, p. 75.

50. Staggenborg 1991, pp. 29–30.

51. Luker 1984, pp. 84–85.

52. Ibid., p. 87. Despite this, the requirement that tests be done to determine whether any fetal indications were present before an abortion

was performed was dropped as a concession to those opposed to abortion, who considered the inclusion of a fetal-indications clause to be deeply offensive.

53. The following discussion is based on Jain and Sinding 1968.

54. Ibid., p. 50.

55. This discussion is based on Jain and Gooch 1972, p. 61.

56. The 1965 introduction of a bill that would have allowed a person to be sterilized without his or her consent if judged not legally competent had been strongly opposed by Archbishop Paul J. Hallinan, whose prominence in Atlanta had increased the Church's public profile in Georgia.

57. As Tatalovich and Daynes note, "To the extent that the explicit goal was therapeutic abortion reform, the intellectual debate tended to focus on those narrow issues relevant to that objective. Thus very little notice was given to abortion in terms of a woman's right, though the question of elective abortion lay beneath the surface of the abortion dialogue, particularly in the late 1960s and early 1970s" (1981, p. 92).

58. Clark 1969, pp. 8–9.

59. In 1869, after centuries of discussion over the point at which a fetus has a soul, Pope Pius IX deleted distinctions made by Aristotle and Gratian that distinguished between embryos without souls, which could be aborted, and those with souls, which could not. The pope ruled that any abortion was grounds for excommunication. See Noonan 1970, p. 40, and Harrison 1983, p. 123. See also Mohr 1978, pp. 186–93 and Luker 1984, p. 59.

60. Harrison 1983, Ch. 5.

61. In addition, since the Church later issued statements against craniotomy and abortions performed to end ectopic pregnancies—abortions that only medically trained physicians were likely to perform—the Church put itself at odds with physicians, who considered such abortions to be medically necessary (Luker 1984, p. 59).

62. Mohr 1978, pp. 184–85; Tatalovich and Daynes 1981, pp. 22–23.

63. The Comstock laws, which were passed in the 1870s, prohibited, among other things, the postal circulation of "indecent materials," including information about abortion. In the 1920s the Catholic Church used the laws to bolster its opposition to widening public access to birth-control devices through clinics (Mohr 1978, p. 196). See also Dienes 1972, p. 93. For a history of the birth-control movement, see Reed 1978 and Dienes 1972.

64. On the history of federal family planning since 1945, see Donald Critchlow 1999.

65. In 1966 the National Catholic Welfare Conference released its first statement against government involvement in birth control programs. For a text of the statement, see Dienes 1972, pp. 327–32.

66. Quoted in Benestad and Butler 1981, p. 150.

67. Hertzke 1988, p. 36.

68. Byrnes 1991, p. 55.

69. Ibid., p. 49.

70. *United States Catholic Conference Annual Reports* (Washington, D.C.: The Administrative Board, 1967), pp. 39–41.

71. The bureau considered this alliance a way to shield the Church from charges that it was trying to require the country to adopt its view of abortion. *United States Catholic Conference Annual Reports* (1968, p. 67). On the National Right-to-Life Committee, see Merton 1981, Paige 1983, and Critchlow 1999.

72. Ginsburg 1989, p. 44.

73. Ibid., pp. 42–43.

74. Traina 1975, pp. 16a–16b.

75. Ibid., p. 8.

76. Abbott 1966, p. 253.

77. Traina 1975, p. 8.

78. Drinan cited the results of the 1965 National Opinion Research Center survey as evidence that the majority of Americans did not favor abortions except in certain cases (1967, pp. 177–79).

79. Carmen, cofounder of the CCS in New York, credited Drinan's writings and lectures in helping the group to develop its legal and theological positions on abortion (Carmen and Moody 1973, p. 38).

80. Like Lader and many of the legislators who supported abortion reform, the Reverend Moody had been active in the Democratic reform movement in New York (Lader 1973, p. 44).

81. The Reverend Howard Moody, telephone interview, February 13, 1992.

82. *The New York Times,* May 22, 1967, p. 1.

83. Quoted in "Abortion, Once Upon a Time in America: Before *Roe v. Wade,* an Underground Effort by a Group of Ministers to Help Pregnant Women" (*The Washington Post,* April 26, 1989, p. 1).

84. Beginning in 1966, the groups listed below released statements in favor of change, ranging from legalizing abortions in cases where the woman's life was in danger to the repeal of abortion laws. With the exception of the Unitarians and the Episcopalians, however, they were not politically active on the state level: the Greek Orthodox Archdiocese of North and South America, 1966; the Episcopal Church, 1967; the Southern Baptist Convention, 1971; the Union of American Hebrew Congregations, 1967; the United Church of Christ, 1970; the United Methodist Church, 1970; the United Presbyterian Church, 1972; the

Unitarian Universalist Association, 1968; the Moravian Church of America, 1970.

85. These were Colorado, California, North Carolina, Georgia, and Maryland. Some activists involved in the abortion-reform movement were also interested in population growth, but since the influence of organizations in this field was not as significant as that of women's-liberation and grassroots abortion groups, they are not included here. For a discussion of the role played by such groups as Zero Population Growth, see Staggenborg 1991. See also Critchlow 1999.

3 Gender Identity and Political Mobilization

The political conflict over abortion policy stems partly from competing ideas about the meaning of womanhood. Because opposing interpretations of gender, sexuality, and reproduction are central to the debate over abortion policy, the pre-*Roe* conflict provides a particularly appropriate context to examine the interplay between social and political factors, and how it led to the politicization of gender and to the repeal of abortion laws in the 1970s.

Women's political identity emerged in the years immediately preceding the pre-*Roe* debate largely as a result of their increasing levels of employment, education, and voting, and their emerging consciousness of their second-class status in the public sector.[1] In the early 1960s, political elites, eager to tap this growing bloc of voters, began organizing women on the national and state levels. One of the first issues women cut their teeth on was abortion policy, and it put them and their movement on the map.[2]

Several partisan and institutional developments in the late 1950s laid the foundation for women's political identity in the following decade. Of prime importance was the establishment of the President's Commission on the Status of Women in 1961 and the subsequent creation of chapters on the state level. A few years later, some of the women involved in these chapters joined the National Organization for Women (NOW); by the late 1960s radical feminist groups had emerged as well. Together, these groups shaped pre-*Roe* abortion politics by pooling their resources and creating a variety of communications networks and discourses that succeeded in taking abortion out of the back alleys and placing it on the legislative floor.[3]

Postwar Opportunities

The emergence of women as a political constituency can be traced to the post-war period. The continuing migration of southern blacks to northern cities and the expansion of the suburbs altered the electoral balance between the parties and increased the competition between them for new constituencies. Chief among these potential voting blocs were women, whose rising rates of employment, education, and voting made them particularly attractive to the parties.

Although women began working outside the home in large numbers during World War II, many who worked in war-related industries were fired once the war ended.[4] In the 1950s women entered the labor force in large numbers again and this time stayed. By 1960 they made up roughly one-third of the labor force, up from 25 percent in 1940, the largest increase since 1900.[5] Similarly, women's education levels rose between 1950 and 1968, with women's percentage of bachelor and first professional degrees rising from 24 percent in 1950 to 43.5 percent in 1968.[6]

Women did not go to the polls in large numbers until 1940, when nearly half of them voted. After the war women's voting rates continued to increase. The significance of this was seen in the election results in the 1950s.[7] The 1952 presidential election returns showed women voters preferred the Republicans to the Democrats by a margin of

5 percent. In the 1956 election the gender gap widened to six points between the parties.[8] Throughout his presidency Eisenhower made repeated efforts to cultivate the women's vote by supporting the passage of equal pay legislation and the ratification of the Equal Rights Amendment.[9] He also appointed hundreds of women to commissions and government positions.[10]

The rapid growth of the suburbs was another factor contributing to the changing electoral trends in the post-war period.[11] Federal subsidies for home mortgages through the Veteran's Administration and the Federal Housing Administration program, as well as for highway construction, contributed to the rise in the annual growth rate of the suburbs, which in the 1950s was twice that of the cities. By 1960, the size of the suburban electorate was larger than that of the central cities, a development that became a potential threat to the Democrats because the suburban turnout rate was higher than in the cities where their support was stronger.[12]

The Democratic National Party responded to the gender gap through its Office of Women's Activities. Beginning in 1957 it held a series of symposiums, hosted by Eleanor Roosevelt, to organize suburban women voters. The groups quickly multiplied and were later credited with helping the party trounce the Republicans in the 1958 Congressional elections.[13]

These electoral patterns persuaded Kennedy's advisors to expand their efforts to secure women's votes for his presidential campaign. Tea parties and neighborhood canvasses were organized to generate support for his candidacy as well as to get feedback from young suburban female voters about which issues mattered to them. Based on both groups' concerns about educating their children, Kennedy included education as part of the "New Frontier" platform of his campaign.[14] The 1960 election returns revealed women responded to Kennedy's strategy. A post-election Gallup poll indicated Kennedy received 10% more votes from women between the ages of 21–29. Amongst women ages 30–49, who traditionally voted Republican, Kennedy's support was equal to Nixon's. [15] Once in office, he continued efforts to retain their support.

In 1961, Kennedy appointed Esther Peterson, an AFL-CIO lobbyist, to be director of the languishing Women's Bureau, a division of the Labor Department that had been established in 1918 to promote the welfare of wage-earning women.[16] In the same year, at Peterson's urging, Kennedy established the Presidential Commission on the Status of Women to study ways to bring American women into the public sphere.[17] The commission, which issued its report in October 1963, recommended a broad range of changes, including revamping continuing-education programs to meet the needs of women whose education had been interrupted by marriage, providing more child-care services, and extending equal opportunity for employment.[18]

While the publicity that the report attracted undoubtedly helped mobilize women around the country, the commission also served as a catalyst for specific developments that contributed to the emergence of women as a political force. One was the passage of the Equal Pay Act, the first federal law prohibiting wage discrimination based on sex; it was signed into law in June 1963, a few months before the commission disbanded. Another was the renewed mobilization of the National Federation of Business and Professional Women's Clubs (BPW). Like the Women's Bureau, the BPW had seemed to have a limited future, given its lack of success in attracting new members.[19] In 1963, the BPW followed the lead of Governor Jon Swainson of Michigan, who had established a Commission on the Status of Women in his state, and began a campaign to establish such commissions in every state. This expansion was supported by Esther Peterson, who had earlier recognized the need to continue the work of the Presidential Commission on the Status of Women after it delivered its report.[20]

As women's issues were beginning to get attention, the demand for federal civil-rights legislation was intensifying. In June of 1963 President Kennedy sent Congress a civil-rights bill that, among other things, banned segregation in public accommodations. In the fall of that year the House added Title VII to the bill, which created the Equal Employment Opportunity Commission to investigate charges of discrimination. Women's concerns were acknowledged in February 1964 when sex was included along with race, color, religion, and national origin as a prohibited basis for discrimination in Title VII of the Act.[21]

The significance of the Civil Rights Act for the purposes of women's mobilization was the connection Title VII made between race and sex within the specific context of equal employment opportunity.[22] The need to extend civil-rights protection to blacks had been demonstrated by the civil-rights movement for a decade, but the idea that women were also in need of protection from discrimination was a radical one in 1964. Although the implications were not immediately apparent, the Civil Rights Act gave women's advocates a legal definition of equality in the workplace, and the institutional means, through the Equal Employment Opportunity Commission, to prevent blatant discrimination against women on the job.

The effects of the national and state networks established by the Women's Bureau and the BPW, and the passage of the Civil Rights Act, went beyond electoral politics. In addition to laying the foundation for the emerging women's movement, these networks highlighted the issue of women's inequality and established expectations, thus fulfilling two of the three conditions necessary for a change in consciousness.[23] The third, that a group of people begin to press their claims in terms of rights, was about to begin.

The National Organization for Women

In 1963, Betty Friedan's seminal book *The Feminine Mystique* identified women's collective anger at the circumscribed parameters of their lives, which Friedan called "the problem with no name." As one woman she interviewed said: "I've tried everything women are supposed to do—hobbies, gardening, pickling, canning, being very social with my neighbors, joining the committees, running PTA teas. I can do it all, and I like it, but it doesn't leave you with anything to think about—any feeling of who you are. . . . There's no problem you can even put a name to. But I'm desperate. I begin to feel I have no personality. I'm a server of food and a putter-on of pants and a bedmaker, somebody who can be called on when you want something. But who am I?"[24]

The problem now had a name: unequal opportunity. After *The Feminine Mystique* was published, Friedan began research for a second book in Washington, D.C. There she interviewed women who had been working in the Women's Bureau on the national and state levels, and who were becoming increasingly frustrated by their lack of progress in ending sexual discrimination. Writing about that period, Friedan recalled that "women were able to bring themselves out of the psychological murk to the brink of action; to bring themselves out of housewife isolation and the apologetic timidity it fostered. Coming together with other women, they made up that critical mass that was about to explode. In that unconscious underground, where each one had been operating alone, not even knowing the other existed, how glad, how relieved we were to find and recognize each other."[25]

The underground surfaced at the Third National Conference on the Status of Women in Washington in the summer of 1966. Charges that the Equal Employment Opportunity Commission (EEOC) was not seriously considering women's complaints about job discrimination angered many women, and there was growing dissatisfaction with the direction that the War on Poverty was taking.[26] A central part of the campaign was the Job Corps, a program aimed at employing poor men, whom experts considered the main providers for households. During hearings by the House Committee on Education and Labor in March of 1964, Representative Edith Green had articulated women's concerns and questioned this assumption.

> I will point out that one out of three persons who today hold jobs in the United States is a woman. Furthermore, there are millions of women who are heads of families, yet they are paid less and they are given fewer opportunities. . . . We dare not suggest that the Job Corps be designed for individuals of a particular race or a particular creed. But this being a man's world we unthinkingly design the Job Corps for men only. . . . It strikes in me an odd chord that, when we have a long-term basic remedial program, women are excluded from a vital section.[27]

To gain Green's support for the bill, the sponsors agreed to include women under their own program, but later limited women's participation in the Jobs Corps to less than a third.[28]

The last straw for women's rights was the EEOC's retreat from abolishing sex-segregated job listings in newspapers.[29] Angered by a rumor that Richard Graham, a member of the EEOC who favored enforcing antidiscrimination laws, was not going to be reappointed, a group of women attending the meeting attempted to introduce a resolution concerning the EEOC's recent ruling on job advertising and its limited efforts in fighting sexual discrimination.[30] After being denied access to the floor, they met with Betty Friedan, who was attending as a writer-observer, and together they formed the National Organization for Women.[31] Many of the early activists who joined NOW had read Friedan's book. One woman recalled that *The Feminine Mystique* "hit me like a bomb."[32]

A central goal of NOW was to introduce a new identity for women based on rights, and to mobilize women to secure it:

> There is no civil rights movement to speak for women, as there has been for Negroes and other victims of discrimination. The National Organization for Women must therefore begin to speak.
>
> WE BELIEVE that the power of American law, and the protection guaranteed by the U. S. Constitution to the civil rights of all individuals, must be effectively applied and enforced to isolate and remove patterns of sex discrimination, to ensure equality of opportunity in employment and education, and equality of civil and political rights and responsibilities on behalf of women, as well as for Negroes and other deprived groups.
>
> WE BELIEVE THAT women will do most to create a new image of women by acting now, and by speaking out in behalf of their own equality, freedom and human dignity. . . . in an active and self-respecting partnership with men.[33]

By identifying themselves as a group that was sexually discriminated against, women such as these framed the problem within the context of women's rights, thus completing the final step needed to go from talk to action.[34]

Networks and Resources

Although NOW was conceived as a national organization, most of its early activity was on the state and local level. This was due to lack of organization and money, and to members' recognition that a decentralized structure could make better use of the spontaneous and grassroots nature of the emerging movement. Within a year, its membership had grown from thirty members to 300.[35] In 1968, NOW had fourteen local chapters; by 1972 it had more than 200.[36] As the largest organization in the late 1960s devoted to securing women's rights, NOW, through its chapters across the country, played a significant role in bringing women together and subsequently in creating a network of activists.

In the late 1960s, some women who had been involved in the civil-rights and antiwar movements became active in the newly emerging women's movement and joined NOW; others formed more radical women's-liberation groups, such as Redstockings, which was established in 1969. Despite their political differences, they shared an antipathy for sexual assumptions that prevented women from achieving economic, social, and political equality.[37] Both wings of the movement generated consciousness-raising groups, a practice some activists had seen in the civil-rights movement.

In its manifesto, Redstockings described the purpose of consciousness-raising: "We regard our personal experiences, and our feelings about that experience, as the basis for an analysis of our common situation. . . . Our chief task at present is to develop female class consciousness through sharing experience and publicly exposing the sexist foundation of all our institutions. Consciousness-raising is not 'therapy,' which implies the existence of individual solutions and falsely assumes that the male-female relationship is purely personal, but the only method by which we can ensure that our program for liberation is based on the concrete realities of our lives."[38]

By challenging and redefining traditional roles, the consciousness-raising sessions led to a change in how women perceived themselves, both socially and politically. The very factor that provoked the prejudice they encountered, namely their gender, became the central element of their political identity. By 1969, nearly fifty consciousness-raising groups had been organized by women's-liberation groups; in 1970 various NOW chapters across the country also established groups.[39] By 1971, the number of consciousness-raising groups was 150.[40]

In addition to mobilizing women to join the movement, the meetings were a catalyst for an increasing number of women to act, either through established means such as lobbying and voting or by participating in more confrontational tactics, such as demonstrations and marches. The range of women that NOW and radical groups drew together into the women's movement brought a combination of inside and outside resources, such as legislative experience and experience in organizing protests. This combination, though it generated discord, strengthened the movement by increasing the number of issues addressed and providing incentives for more women to join.[41]

The beginning of the women's movement coincided with the emergence of pro-abortion campaigns across the nation. Gradually, a discourse coalition on abortion developed that included women active in the movement and women working for abortion reform. This was almost inevitable, due to the grassroots nature of NOW and the various abortion groups across the country. Often they attracted the same small segment of politically active people in a given community. Although some pro-abortion activists did not join NOW, and some women active in the movement were more concerned with pay equity and the equal-rights amendment, a sufficient number of them were active in both. As one activist in Philadelphia put it, "We were all the same people—we just wore different hats sometimes."[42]

An example of the pre-*Roe* alliance that grew between pro-abortion activists and NOW in New York is described by Constance Cook, a Republican Assemblywoman and an early member of NOW, who cosponsored the 1970 New York repeal bill. In an interview in 1976, Cook told how NOW was able to make use of a list of women's organizations put together by the Women's Division of the New York State Fair. "The Fair runs an extensive operation with all the women's groups throughout the state," Cook said. "At that time [1969] it was even more active than it is now." The president of the Women's Division gave Cook the list, "and on top of that, she helped us to get feedback on who was active, who was responsible, who would follow through . . . where our friends were. . . . And the first thing I did . . . I sent it to Betty Friedan. She wanted to know how you organize women in this state."[43]

Faux's analysis of the pre-*Roe* campaign in Texas illustrates another dimension of the relationships among women who were politically active around feminist issues in the 1960s. According to Faux, the moderates "were sympathetic to some degree because they knew politics had played a major role in delaying long-overdue reform in New York, but they felt their reform effort was moving along more smoothly in Texas because they had not couched their argument in feminist terms. Texas feminists were increasingly making themselves heard on the subject of abortion, and the Dallas reformers were growing alarmed. Philosophically, they stood shoulder to shoulder with the feminists; tactically, they were miles apart."[44]

The pre-*Roe* campaigns proved to be ideal vehicles for uniting women, because restrictive abortion laws affected them as few other issues did; the issue was something that almost all women could relate to. In addition to impeding their upward mobility in the workplace, these laws posed a direct threat to women who worked at home, by limiting their ability to control their reproductive lives. The calls for abortion reform and repeal resonated with thousands of women who had had illegal abortions and with many others who had endured the humiliation of appearing before a hospital board to plead their case.[45] Although their positions on abortion ranged from calls for limited reform to demands for outright repeal, the discourse coalitions emerging in various states were united by feminist ideas concerning women's liberty, in the home and on the job.[46]

Feminist and Legal Discourses

With the adoption of the ALI laws beginning in 1966, pro-reform forces had succeeded in giving poor as well as rich women greater access to therapeutic abortions. A central component of their argument was that the existing laws violated poor women's right to equality and should be changed so that any woman who qualified for a therapeutic abortion should receive one, regardless of her economic status.[47] Throughout this period, however, thousands of women who wanted abortions were forced to obtain illegal ones because their pregnancies were not covered by the ALI

provisions. Radical feminists, who were increasingly dissatisfied with the narrow definitions of the ALI laws, took the
next step by creating an abortion-repeal discourse that incorporated the concepts of equality and autonomy within
that of choice.[48]

The privacy argument articulated in *Griswold* in the context of contraception supported the feminists' claim that
reproductive control was a matter of individual liberty. They
argued that since women were the individuals who became
pregnant, laws that prohibited their access to abortion, as
well as to contraceptives, were unconstitutional because
they violated women's Fourteenth Amendment rights to
liberty and property, which included both the right to privacy and the control of one's body.[49] By defining access to
contraception and abortion as a reproductive right within
the broader context of choice, feminists framed the *Griswold*
decision in terms of sex, and argued that any woman,
regardless of income or reason, had the right to have an
abortion without interference.

It was the radical feminists' calls for "abortion on
demand" that moved the campaign to the next step. Though
this was only one part of the feminists' agenda, it was considered by some activists to be "the thing that would appeal
to most people, most women [because] in the course of
their lives, every single woman has probably had a chance
or thought about an abortion. . . . We felt the demand would
bring more people in. . . ."[50] Their calls for repeal laid the
foundation for a coalition based on a feminist definition of
rights, which challenged established medical, religious, and
political positions on abortion, and incorporated parts of an
emerging legal discourse that questioned the states' role in
the area of reproductive freedom.[51]

In the late 1960s, state courts in California, Pennsylvania, and the District of Columbia used the concept of privacy articulated in *Griswold* as the basis of decisions to include access to abortion as part of the right to privacy protected by the Constitution. In *People v. Belous,* the California Supreme Court stated that

> the rights involved in the instant case are the woman's rights to life and to choose whether to bear children. . . . The fundamental right of the woman to choose whether to bear children follows from the Supreme Court's and this court's repeated acknowledgement of a "right of privacy" or "liberty" in matters related to marriage, family and sex. . . . That such a right is not enumerated in either the United States or California Constitutions is no impediment to the existence of the right. . . . The critical issue here is not whether such rights exist, but whether the state has a compelling interest in the regulation of a subject which is within the police powers of the state. . . .[52]

Belous was the first decision to give legal sanction to feminists' interpretation of the "individual's" right to privacy concerning contraceptives to mean a "woman's" right. In effect, by explicitly making this connection between rights and access to abortion, *Belous* laid the legal foundation for the repeal of restrictive abortion laws. Two months later, a woman's right to control her reproductive function was cited in *United States v. Vuitch:* "There has been . . . an increasing indication in decisions of the Supreme Court of the United States that as a secular matter a woman's liberty and right of privacy extends to family, marriage and sex matters and may well include the right to remove an unwanted child at least in the early stages of pregnancy."[53]

Two women attorneys involved in similar suits recalled the atmosphere of the courts at the time:

When we came into court three years ago with all of this
[1970], the judges didn't have the foggiest notion of what
we were talking about and many male lawyers treated us as
unwanted interlopers. I mean, they really did not understand
women's rights claims and they certainly did not understand
how serious it was for a woman to have an unwanted child.
The degree of the progression of the opinions was extraordi-
nary in a period which I consider fairly short, given the nov-
elty of the fundamental rights we are talking about here.
I think that was extremely impressive. But again I must stress
that I think the progression was largely due to the strategy of
bringing women's rights cases. I don't think we could have
educated the judges the same way in purely doctors' lawsuits.[54]

The rulings in *Belous* and *Vuitch* extended the argument
in *Griswold*. Whereas *Griswold* had determined that the states
had no constitutional basis to interfere with a married couple's right to procure contraceptives, *Belous* and *Vuitch* applied this right to cover a woman's decision to have an abortion. In each opinion, the right to privacy established in
Griswold was acknowledged to be part of the larger issue of
state regulation of family matters. Hence, within a four-year
period, the compelling interests of the states to prohibit the
sale of contraceptives and the practice of most abortions
had been superseded by women's rights to early abortions.[55]

These decisions encouraged local feminist groups to
adopt litigation strategies, and by 1970 similar suits had
been brought in several other states.[56] In Illinois, activist
attorneys challenged the constitutionality of a state statute
that prohibited all abortions except when the woman's life
was in danger.[57] The case, *Doe v. Scott,* was significant both for
the circumstances of its plaintiffs and for its arguments.[58]

The plaintiffs included a rich woman who had obtained
an abortion abroad after being denied one in Illinois, a poor

woman who could not afford to travel and was forced to bear her child after being denied an abortion, and several physicians who claimed that the statute interfered with their ability to practice medicine by subjecting them to possible prosecution.[59] By representing physicians and women together, the lawyers arguing the case were able not only to challenge the statute on the usual grounds of vagueness, broadness, and privacy, but to illustrate the inherent class bias of restrictive laws, which fell disproportionately upon poor women.[60] In its decision, the court spoke to this point:

> Aside from the fact that the statute is vague, its practical effect is to make abortion unavailable to women unless there is a reasonable certainty that death will result from a continuation of pregnancy. This practical effect of the statute constitutes an intrusion on constitutionally protected areas too sweeping to be justified as necessary to accomplish any compelling state interest. These protected areas are women's rights to life, to control over their own bodies, and to privacy and freedom in matters relating to sex and procreation. . . . Moreover, a statute which forces the birth of every fetus, no matter how defective or how intensely unwanted by its future parents, displays no legitimately compelling state interest in fetal life, especially when viewed with regard for the countervailing rights of the pregnant woman.[61]

In New York, a coalition of women's groups, the Community Action Legal Services Office, physicians, and abortion activists filed four suits challenging the abortion statute on several grounds, including constitutionality and the infringement of medical practice.[62] Although the New York abortion law was repealed before the cases went to trial, and the Illinois decision was immediately appealed, the lawyers arguing both cases incorporated legal and medical discourses and grounded them in a feminist framework. Another of the primary purposes of these cases—educating the public and the courts about abortion and other women's issues—was also accomplished.

As significant as both cases were in raising public consciousness about women's-rights issues, the 1970 case of *Babbitz v. McCann* was even important because the federal court panel based its decision on the Ninth Amendment, the foundation of *Griswold,* instead of on the usual grounds of vagueness and due process: "Under its police power, the state can regulate certain aspects of abortion. Thus, it is permissible for the state to require that abortions be conducted by qualified physicians. The police power of the state does not, however, entitle it to deny a woman the basic right reserved to her under the Ninth amendment to decide whether she should carry or reject an embryo which has not yet quickened. The challenged sections of the present Wisconsin law suffer from an infirmity of fatal overbreadth."[63]

Equally important, the court cited the common-law distinction of quickening as the balancing point between a woman's right to privacy and a fetus's right to life: "The defendants urge that the state's interest in protecting the embryo is a sufficient basis to sustain the statute. Upon a balancing of the relevant interests, we hold that a woman's right to refuse to carry an embryo during the early months of pregnancy may not be invaded by the state without a more compelling public necessity than is reflected in the statute in question. . . . When measured against the claimed 'rights' of an embryo of four months or less, we hold that the mother's right transcends that of such an embryo."[64]

In the same year as the *Babbitz* decision was handed down, feminists in New York were engaged in a legislative campaign that accelerated the abortion debate and set the stage for the rancorous battles that followed.

Notes

1. For a discussion of the factors that contributed to women's politicization in the postwar period, see Klein 1984, Ferris 1971, Freeman 1975, and Zelman 1980.

2. Like any other constituency, women as a group are by no means united. For example, women committed to women's equality from a rights-based approach differed from those who were in favor of abolishing sex roles, and liberating women from them. Generally speaking, women's-rights advocates sought to reform society through established means, such as legislation and court cases; women's-liberation activists sought to change it outside these established channels. I use the term "women's movement" to describe both groups because I am more interested in how each wing shaped the strategies and goals of the abortion campaigns in the pre-*Roe* period than in the ideological and political differences between them. See Hole and Levine 1971 and Ryan 1992.

3. Of course, activism cuts both ways. In Chapter Five I analyze the success of antiabortion forces in Pennsylvania.

4. Chafe 1972, p. 148.

5. Silverberg 1988, p. 37.

6. Freeman 1975, p. 29.

7. By 1968, women's rate of voting (66 percent) was comparable to men's (69 percent). See Klein 1984, p. 143.

8. Costain 1992, p. 33

9. Ibid.

10. Ibid., p. 34.

11. Silverberg 1988, p. 39. The following discussion of the mobilization of suburban women is based extensively on Silverberg, Ch.2

12. Ibid., pp. 39–41.

13. Ibid., p. 43.

14. Ibid., p. 47.

15. Ibid., p. 50.

16. Freeman 1975, pp. 208–9.

17. In the early 1960s, sex had not yet become politicized, and Kennedy was no more interested in women's educational and professional opportunities than anyone else. Female voters were just another constituency he needed to balance the increasing support Republicans were gaining in the suburbs. Although Peterson's position on protective labor legislation and the equal-rights amendment differed from the party's and Kennedy's positions, Kennedy supported her for reasons explained by Zelman 1980, Ch. 2. Also see Deckard 1983.

18. Hole and Levine 1971, pp. 433–36.

19. Silverberg 1988, p. 70.

20. East 1983, p. 35. See also Silverberg 1988, p. 72. Peterson proposed expanding and decentralizing the Women's Bureau so that it could mobilize groups of women on the state and local levels to work on pay discrimination and equal educational opportunity.

21. The following description of the politics of Title VII and the EEOC is taken from Zelman 1980, Ch. 4. This reference is on p. 67.

22. Ibid., Ch. 4.

23. Piven and Cloward 1977, pp. 4–5.

24. Quoted in Friedan 1963, p. 21.

25. Quoted in Friedan 1985, p. 76.

26. Zelman 1980, p. 94. See also Freeman 1975, Ch. 2.

27. Zelman 1980, p. 81.

28. Ibid., p. 84.

29. Copies of Representative Martha Griffith's speech on the House floor, denouncing the EEOC's position, were circulating at the conference, and also added fuel to the controversy (Freeman 1975, p. 54,).

30. Zelman 1980, pp. 101–6

31. Freeman 1975, p. 54. See also Friedan 1985, p. 83.

32. Carden 1974, p. 155.

33. Carabillo et al. 1993, pp. 161–62.

34. Piven and Cloward 1977, p. 4, For various theories of why the women's movement emerged in the late 1960s, see Ryan 1992, Echols 1989, Freeman 1975, Hole and Levine 1971, and Costain 1992.

35. Carden 1974, p. 105.

36. Echols 1989, p. 83. See also Hole and Levine 1971, Ch. 2.

37. One indication of this can be seen in both groups' efforts to use the news media to shape the public discourse on a wide range of issues affecting women, including abortion policy. See Silverberg, pp. 110–15. See Hole and Levine 1971 for a discussion of various feminist groups in this period. For an example of the range of women writing on feminist topics at the time, see Morgan 1970. On birth control, see Cisler (in Morgan 1970, pp. 254–89).

38. Quoted in Hole and Levine 1971, p. 138.

39. Carden 1974, pp. 64, 107.

40. Deckard 1983, p. 326.

41. Ryan 1992, pp. 45–46.

42. Winnie Shoeffer, a member of PARA and CHOICE, telephone interview, January 6, 1993.

43. Family Planning Oral History Project Records, 1976, pp. 50–51.

44. Faux 1988, p. 201.

45. In the course of writing this book I met dozens of women of all ages and political persuasions who described their anger and resentment over the obstacles they had to overcome to get an abortion. For example, one way to get an abortion, commonly used by women who were not the victims of a crime or who were not carrying a deformed fetus, was to obtain a certification from two psychiatrists that the pregnancy imperiled the woman's mental health. Another was to appear before a hospital board of physicians and explain why an abortion was necessary.

46. Although a few early groups, such as the Citizens' Committee for Humane Abortion Laws and Illinois Citizens for the Medical Control of Abortion, favored repeal, most groups were committed to reform in the 1960s, until radical feminists began to challenge this position.

47. For an excellent analysis of the development of pre-*Roe* rhetoric, see Condit (Ch. 2–4). This reference is on page 64. Reagan makes a similar observation in her analysis of the motivation of the attorneys who brought the *Doe v. Scott* case to trial (Reagan 1997, p. 236).

48. As Condit notes, some radical feminists opposed the use of the term "choice" because it did not take into account women who lacked the money to sue to have an abortion. See Condit 1990, pp. 67–68.

49. This is not to say that no distinction was made between contraception and abortion, but rather that both were reproductive issues, and that if access to contraception was constitutionally protected, was it not logical that access to abortion should be as well?

50. Quoted in Staggenborg 1991, p. 45.

51. For the history of the Connecticut campaign to legalize the dissemination of birth-control information before *Poe v. Ullman*, see Garrow 1994, Ch. 1–3. See also Westin 1967 and Redlich 1962. In addition, in the late 1960s several law-review articles argued that there was a constitutional right to abortion. Articles by Lucas (1968), Means (1968, 1971), and Clark (1969) are discussed in Chapter Two.

52. *People v. Belous*, 71 Cal. 2d 954, 458 P. 2d 194 (1969), at 199–200.

53. *United States v. Vuitch*, 350 F. Supp. 1032 (D.D.C. 1969), at 1035.

54. Quoted in Rubin 1987, pp. 47–48. For cases filed as of 1972, see Vertaga et al. 1972.

55. The majority of abortions are performed in the first trimester of pregnancy.

56. By 1970, thirteen states had suits pending. *Congressional Quarterly Fact Sheet* (24 July 1970): 1913. For a discussion of federal cases, see Sigworth 1971, pp. 130–42.

57. *Doe v. Scott*, 321 F. Supp. 1385 (1971).

58. See Reagan's analysis of this case, pp. 235–40.

59. Joining them in the suit was Mary Poe, representing her under-age daughter Pauline Poe, as Intervening Plaintiff.

60. The attorneys in the case argued that the law "systematically discriminates against poor women, depriving them of equal access to the treatment available to women of means solely because they are poor" (quoted in Reagan 1997, p. 236).

61. *Doe v. Scott*, 321 F. Supp. 1385: at 1389, 1391.

62. *Abramowicz v. Lefkowitz*, 305 F. Supp. 1030 (S.D.N.Y. 1969).

63. *Babbitz v. McCann*, 310 F. Supp. 293 (1970, at 302).

64. *Babbitz* (p. 301).

4 Party Politics in New York

Among the first states to repeal its abortion law in the pre-*Roe* period was New York, which in 1970 joined Hawaii, Alaska, and Washington in legalizing early elective abortions with few restrictions. Unlike Washington, which bypassed the legislative route and its inherent obstacles by holding a referendum on repeal, pro- and antiabortion forces in New York fought it out on the legislative floor for four years. New York had the largest and most diverse ethnic and religious population in the country, as well one of the most powerful Catholic Conferences. Yet of the four states' bills, New York's had the fewest restrictions, thus making it the purest repeal bill.

In his book about the early days of the abortion campaign, Lader maintains that "it was partly a movement of chance and almost reckless determination, for there was little logical reason that all the necessary pieces should fit together in 1965 rather than 25 years later."[1] This observation captures the volatility of political change from the perspective of an activist. But to fully understand why pro-abortion activists succeeded, it is also necessary to analyze the changes in the party structure in New York and the resulting opportunities and resources activists encountered.

Pre-*Roe* abortion policy in New York developed in two distinct stages. In the first stage (1965–67), ALI-based abortion reform laws were introduced and defeated. In the second stage (1968–70), changes in the New York Legislature and the New York Catholic Conference (NYCC), coupled with feminists' demand for unrestricted access to abortion, enabled pro-abortion activists use the support they had built to push for repeal.

The First Stage: 1965–1967

The Push for Reform

In 1964, pro-abortion activists in New York took their first step in organizing support for change by forming the Committee for a Humane Abortion Law, later renamed the Association for the Study of Abortion. A survey taken in that year indicated that obstetricians in New York supported abortion reform, yet the idea was still controversial.[2] Like other early pro-reform groups, such as the California Committee on Therapeutic Abortion, the association lent legitimacy to the fledgling campaign because its members included physicians, theologians, lawyers, and other elites. It was thus able to press into service elements of all the relevant discourses at the time. The group began a public campaign to promote reform by sponsoring films, writing letters to obstetrics departments in medical schools, printing brochures and quarterly newsletters, creating mailing lists, and contacting foundations.[3]

Members' efforts were bolstered the following year by the *Griswold* decision. Although encouraged, activists realized that using the decision to challenge restrictive abortion laws would take several years, and would require a physician who was willing to break the law and risk professional ruin.[4] For this reason, they decided to broaden their efforts by embarking on a legislative campaign to pass new laws. The positive reception they received at a public forum on reform sponsored by the Yorkville Democratic Club in 1965 led to the introduction of the first abortion-reform bill later in the year by Assemblyman Percy Sutton and Senator Manfred Ohrenstein, both downstate reform Democrats.[5]

Like reform bills introduced in other states in this period, the New York law was based on the American Law Institute's guidelines. At the bill's hearing in March of 1966, held by the Assembly Committee on Health, abortion activists and members of the Liberal Party and the New York Young Democratic Party testified in its favor.[6] The NYCC considered the bill's chances of making it out of committee so slim that it did not send a representative to testify against it.[7] Although the bill died in committee, the hearing was covered on the front page of *The New York Times,* introducing the idea to an audience outside the reform clubs and activist circles.

After the bill's defeat, Assemblyman Albert Blumenthal, a reform Democrat from Manhattan, agreed to sponsor a second reform bill the following year.[8] Blumenthal's interest in abortion stemmed from his general concern with issues of public health, and as chairman of the Assembly Committee on Health, he framed abortion as a public-health issue.[9] Blumenthal's bill incorporated the ALI-based sections of the Sutton bill and added the requirement that a committee of physicians be established to approve all abortions performed in a hospital. In an effort to get the bill out of committee and onto the floor for debate in 1967, several organizations sponsored a petition drive in support of the bill.[10] Despite this, it was defeated in the Assembly Codes Committee, 15 to 3.

During this early period, the chief opponent of abortion reform, the NYCC, was occupied with other issues, primarily building support to repeal the Blaine amendment, an article of the state Constitution that prohibited the use of public funds for parochial schools.[11] Nonetheless, it issued a press release to the Catholic press in January 1967 against reform, and responded to the petition drive by issuing a pastoral letter, which was read at hundreds of Catholic churches around the state. It read in part: "The purpose of this joint pastoral letter is to invite your most serious reflection on our position as Catholics regarding the right to life of every human being and our consequent opposition to abortion. . . . Since laws which allow abortion violate the unborn child's God-given right, we are opposed to any proposal to extend them. We urge you most strongly to do all in your power to prevent direct attacks upon the lives of unborn children."[12]

The Protestant Council and the Federation of Reform Synagogues of New York protested the NYCC's involvement in the political debate over abortion policy, but the NYCC was undeterred.[13]

A few weeks before the pastoral letter was made public, Blumenthal was ousted from his post as chairman of the Democratic Advisory Committee, a policy-steering committee that had been created in 1966 by Anthony Travia, Speaker of the Assembly. Except for Blumenthal, all the members of the committee were regular, as opposed to reform, Democrats. According to Travia, Blumenthal was removed because of pressure from the other members, who feared the electoral consequences of his positions on abortion and other issues.[14] Pressure from the NYCC, as well as the ongoing struggle between reformers and party regulars, undoubtedly contributed to Travia's decision.[15]

Grassroots Activism

It was at this point, in May 1967, that the Reverend Howard Moody and other clergy members opened the Clergy Consultation Service. Although the CCS challenged the Catholic Church's role as the exclusive moral and religious authority on the abortion issue in a way no other group could, Moody recalled that it never came under any pressure from the Church to curtail its activities.[16] Given the NYCC's ability to kill reform bills in committee, the CCS posed no legislative threat in this first stage of the conflict. However, in the same way that the Association for the Study of Abortion had helped to legitimize the public debate about abortion reform, the establishment of the CCS encouraged other organizations to join the emerging coalition. Aryeh Neier, director of the New York chapter of the American Civil Liberties Union, credited the CCS with mobilizing his members. The group, Neier said, "challenged the political sanctions and put itself on the line. It helped to take [abortion reform] out of the shadows and made it a respectable issue."[17]

Other groups joined as well.[18] The most active of these was the Organization for Abortion Law Reform (OALR) founded by John Lassoe. Lassoe was the legislative liaison in Albany for the New York Episcopal Diocese, and a member of the legislative committee of the New York State Council of Churches.[19] Before working for the Episcopalians, Lassoe had been active in the civil-rights movement. Like others who became involved with the pro-abortion campaign, he was influenced by Howard Moody, and he believed that the current abortion restrictions were unjust.[20]

According to Lassoe, the OALR was a "paper organization" that provided a loose structure for meetings of people from various medical and legal groups to discuss the issue.[21]

This lack of organizational structure reflected the early days of the reform campaign, when individuals often played a more significant role than the organizations they represented.[22] This was true because there were few established organizations actively promoting abortion reform, and because a formal challenge to the opponents of reform had not yet been mounted.

The New York Episcopal Diocese was behind Lassoe's efforts from the start, probably because it viewed the abortion controversy as a pretext to directly challenge the Catholic Church's use of the issue to increase its political influence, especially while the Church was trying to repeal the Blaine amendment. In 1967 the Episcopal Diocese of Albany issued a position paper on therapeutic abortion, endorsed by the Diocesan Department of Christian Social Relations and the Diocesan Council, in support of the ALI model code.[23] Lassoe used his position as liaison for the New York diocese to create support for abortion reform, speaking at meetings of Episcopal women's church groups and participating in the New York State Council of Churches.

Following the death of Cardinal Francis Spellman in 1967, the selection of Cardinal Terence Cooke to replace Spellman marked a change in leadership at the NYCC that would later have significant repercussions in the New York campaign. Cooke's appointment reflected the new approach to social issues endorsed by Vatican II, a view that was more collective and tolerant of opposing views.[24] In this early period, Cooke, unlike Spellman, was not interested in politics and did not seek to influence Catholic legislators.[25] He was more pastoral in his approach to the diocese and more concerned with expanding services to the poor and the elderly.[26] Although Charles Tobin, the secretary of the NYCC, continued to direct the conference's legislative platform after Spellman's death, the group's authority began to decrease.

Assemblywoman Constance Cook later said that "the Catholic political operation in Albany has long been very potent and powerful, and I think it had, shall we say, slid, relaxed, gotten maybe old and weak in a way . . . and the old type of discipline that used to exist with respect to Catholic legislators simply didn't exist."[27]

While these internal changes were taking place within the NYCC, in 1967 the New York State Right-to-Life Committee was formed by Ed Golden, a Catholic construction foreman, along with a few friends from the Christian Family Movement, a small group that Golden met with to talk about family and church issues. Like most people, Golden had not thought about abortion as a political issue until Albert Blumenthal introduced his first abortion-reform bill in the 1966–67 legislative session.[28] Charles Tobin of the NYCC, recognizing the value of having a group outside the Church lobbying against abortion reform, encouraged his efforts.[29]

Although the New York State Right-to-Life Committee disagreed with the Church's prohibition of contraception, Golden recognized the NYCC as a natural ally: "We talked it over ourselves before we went anywhere near our churches, and what we wanted from them was not direction, or even support, but information we could use in the fight. And that's the way we have continued to operate. I am not saying that we haven't accepted assistance from the churches, in helping us organize, or even in political races—if it was offered in a prudent fashion—but we are the last people to go to the churches and ask their help."[30] Similarly, the NYCC did not consider the committee central to its effort to stop the pro-abortion activists, and it met with Golden only sporadically. In its first year, Golden's group operated on a budget of approximately $400 and spent most of its time urging members to write letters opposing abortion to legislators and local newspapers.[31] By 1968, the group was well enough organized to testify against the second Blumenthal reform bill.

Meanwhile, pro-abortion activists continued working with the reform Democrats. They concentrated on creating a broad coalition of religious, political, and grassroots groups committed to promoting reform. As the campaign moved into its second stage, however, it changed its course and framing strategy, reflecting the participation of radical feminists and other grassroots groups that favored a more fundamental change.

The Second Stage: 1968–1970

From Reform to Repeal

In the spring of 1968, pro-abortion forces succeeded in getting Blumenthal's second abortion-reform bill out of the Assembly Codes Committee and onto the floor. After five hours of debate, Blumenthal recommitted the bill before the roll call was finished to avoid a major defeat.[32] The absence of sufficient support to pass even a moderate reform bill, as several other states had already done, mobilized the more radical elements of the pro-abortion coalition to push for repeal.[33]

From the start of the campaign in 1965, some pro-abortion activists had supported outright repeal, but given the history of restrictive abortion laws and the climate of silence these laws had created, repeal seemed hopelessly unrealistic and likely to create a backlash against moderate reform. As Constance Cook remarked, "Most people were going for reform, as you know, on the theory that half a loaf is better than none."[34] The hearings on Blumenthal's reform bills were critical in breaking the silence about reform, but by 1968 it was becoming increasingly evident that the main problem was the concept of reform. Abortion-reform supporters could not agree on the reasons for therapeutic abortions. Some approved of abortions in cases where pregnancy was the result of a crime, but not when fetal deformities were likely; others questioned the validity of mental-health reasons. These differences played into the hands of the NYCC, which held that life begins at conception and equated all abortions, for whatever reason, with murder.

It became clear that to bring about legislative change it would be necessary to replace the medical and moral definitions of abortion with a political one that could unite all reform supporters. Only a coalition based on limited repeal could accomplish this, because it would provide greater latitude for differences and could incorporate the discourses favored by physicians, attorneys, and most feminists.[35] By requiring that only licensed physicians perform abortions, a limited repeal bill would give physicians the legal protection they needed to perform abortions and would buttress their claims that abortion was a medical issue. Such a bill would include the rights-based approach to abortion introduced by *Griswold,* which lawyers and civil-rights activists favored, and would support their arguments that abortion was a legal issue. It would unite reformers who disagreed with the Church's highly restrictive policy but who also opposed radical feminists' demands for the complete repeal of abortion laws. In effect, the repeal position satisfied the interests of all the major pro-abortion players, with the exception of the radical feminists.[36]

While this debate was taking place, several other developments facilitated the shift to repeal. After a public-opinion poll taken in New York in December 1967 indicated high levels of support for reform among Catholics and non-Catholics alike, Governor Nelson Rockefeller, who had not publicly supported reform, followed public sentiment and announced his support for changes in the abortion law.[37] The following month, to give himself more room to maneuver, he created the Governor's Commission to study the issue of reform. The religious diversity of the commission's members—four Catholics, three Jews, and four Protestants—challenged the Catholic Church's claim of exclusive moral authority on the issue and preempted accusations of religious bias.[38]

The 1968 New York legislative elections also brought a change in leadership. Unlike his predecessor, Anthony Travia, the new Speaker of the Assembly, Perry Duryea, was a Republican who supported abortion reform. Though the Republican majority leader, Earl Brydges, opposed reform, he suspected that it was inevitable, especially in light of Rockefeller's support. The inability of the NYCC to kill abortion reform in committee as it had done in the past, and the split within the Republican leadership over reform, were early indications that the political climate in Albany was changing.[39] Another sign was the decision of Constance Cook to take over the legislative campaign.

After the Blumenthal bill was recommitted in 1968, Ruth Cusak, a member of the National Organization for Women, wrote to Cook, an influential Republican legislator, and asked her to sponsor a repeal bill.[40] Cook agreed for several reasons. She thought the reform strategy was misguided, and although she was doubtful that a repeal bill would pass, she considered it worth supporting. The legislative changes and the formation of Rockefeller's commission helped to convince Cook that she could mobilize sufficient support within the Assembly to introduce repeal.[41] She had also been contacted by an upstate contingent of the Clergy Consultation Service, whose commitment to abortion reform had made a favorable impression on her.[42]

Cook was also a feminist. She had attended an early meeting of NOW at Betty Friedan's apartment to discuss how to mobilize women politically in the state, and she joined National NOW in 1967.[43] The feminist aspect of the issue influenced her decision to carry the bill. She was angered by the reform speeches, which she characterized as "so outrageous, and so male-oriented that I decided, 'Oh, I'd love to show them what a real bill is. If they think this is bad, they should really get a bill.' And that did set my mind, I must say, to introduce outright repeal."[44]

Despite these legislative developments, the NYCC did not alter its strategy after the 1968 election. Based on its past success in containing the debate, the conference assumed it would continue to have the votes to defeat reform, and certainly to crush a repeal bill. As this memo from 1969 shows, the conference continued to lobby against reform but did not attempt to broaden its base or to create grassroots support beyond the Catholic community:

> In the last couple of days we have taken certain action in this office, the fact of which should be brought to the attention of the Coordinators. We have addressed a letter to Assemblyman ... with a copy to all the Legislators reaffirming our opposition to the change in the Abortion Law. With this letter we enclose the pamphlet: "Questions and Answers on Abortion."
>
> We have distributed to the Knights of Columbus at the state level a format for writing letters to the Legislators. The Knights of Columbus will in turn make it available to its various organizations. We also produced some press releases over

the weekend which were made available to all the Catholic newspapers in New York State.[45]

The NYCC's steadfast opposition to any changes in abortion policy, despite public support in favor of limited reform, inadvertently increased the chances of a repeal bill passing because it precluded the possibility of any compromise. Given the Catholic position, however, the conference had little room to maneuver; any changes would have contradicted the position established by Vatican II. Regarded in this light, its policy was consistent, but its strong-arm approach was not in tune with the developments in Albany or the rest of the state.

The Repeal-Discourse Coalition

Once the repeal discourse had been articulated, the next step was to generate sufficient legislative support to enact new laws. In December of 1968, Cook and her cosponsor, Franz Leichter, a freshman reform Democrat from Manhattan, pre-filed the first repeal bill in New York. Their bill would have removed abortion from the criminal code, leaving it under the regulation of the health law, which required that only licensed physicians perform abortions. Neither Cook nor Leichter expected the bill to pass. Rather, they sought to widen the parameters of the debate by challenging the NYCC's moral definition of abortion as murder with a political one that defined abortion repeal as the position supported by the majority.

By taking this course, Cook and Leichter met the NYCC on its own ground; religious opposition to reform was countered by public support for the repeal of abortion restrictions. The repeal position forced the issue: Either abortion was always murder, as the Catholic Conference maintained, or it was not. In the same way that the Blumenthal bills had introduced the idea of reform to a skeptical public, the Cook-Leichter bill was an attempt to get the public to consider repeal seriously.

By 1969, the discourse coalition favoring repeal was slowly emerging among abortion activists in small grassroots groups and various churches and synagogues. Individuals such as Ruth Cusak, whose group affiliations had been preceded by their personal commitments to the issue, played a key role in shaping pre-*Roe* abortion policy.[46] An early supporter of repeal, Cusak wrote her assemblyman, Perry Duryea, in 1967 about introducing a repeal bill. In the same year, she testified in favor of repeal at a public hearing on abortion. There she met Ti-Grace Atkinson, president of New York NOW, who also supported repeal. Atkinson invited her to a NOW meeting and soon persuaded her to head NOW's committee on abortion, most of whose members favored reform. As chairwoman of the committee, Cusak began a letter-writing campaign, using a list supplied by the OALR, to gather organizational support for repeal. Soon afterward, she wrote to Constance Cook and asked her to sponsor a repeal bill. To her amazement, Cook agreed. In December of 1968, Cusak arranged a meeting between Cook and Leichter in Manhattan, where the legislators agreed to cosponsor a repeal bill.

Neither Cook, Cusak, nor Leichter could remember how Leichter came to team up with Cook, but the consensus was that a downstate Democrat was needed to balance Cook's Republican upstate support. Leichter, who was looking for new issues and who supported repeal, fit the bill. Cook did recall the crucial role played by Cusak: "The abortion law was the result of a lot of people's input. Each one at a given time was essential. Without each one, it would never have passed. Well, I think Dr. Ruth [Cusak] was very essential this particular time, because she seemed to be the one that kept plugging on legislative change, to get the bill, to get the sponsors. She got at me, and she got at Franz Leichter."[47]

Typical of the upstate groups was the Committee for Progressive Legislation, an organization based in the Unitarian Church in Albany and Schenectady that worked on a range of issues from criminal justice to abortion. From its start in 1969, the CPL's abortion committee focused on legislative action and spent most of its time lobbying legislators.[48] Trudy Carpenter, one of the regular lobbyists, described their approach as one of "trying to bring them over. Talking about family planning, trying to show them the contradiction about being for family planning but being against abortion."[49]

The approximately thirty active members of the CPL met to lobby each Tuesday of the legislative session after the weekly Legislative Forum meetings, where legislators answered questions about upcoming bills. In Albany, they were in regular contact with Mary Anne Krupsak, their assemblywoman, whose office they used as a meeting place, and with Constance Cook, who gave them lists of legislators to meet with.

According to Cook, the value of small meetings between a handful of constituents and a legislator was crucial to the bill's passage: "Our objective was a simple one. First of all, we wanted to know the position of every single legislator in the state, so that meant we had to get a constituent to talk to him. He would tell me one thing . . . but he might tell his constituents something else. They're the only ones who have the ability to pin him down. To hold him responsible. . . .

So we would get a group, usually three or four prominent constituents if we could, to go to their legislator, and say, 'how do you feel about abortion repeal? What's your position? This is our position.' And they'd try to pin him down. Then we'd start running a list [of legislators]."[50]

The CPL brought together people from several community and social-service organizations, creating a grassroots network of pro-repeal activists.[51] In November of 1969, it held an all-day workshop in Schenectady to organize support for the Cook-Leichter bill. In addition to asking people to write to legislators, the CPL laid plans to organize pro-repeal groups in four surrounding towns; these groups would contact local groups and work with them to pressure undecided legislators to support the bill.[52] While the legislature was in session, the CPL mailed a monthly newsletter to all the Unitarian parishes in the state, asking members to write to their legislators in support of abortion repeal and to lobby with the CPL in Albany.[53]

The CPL accepted help from women in other groups, including Planned Parenthood and the League of Women Voters. One such woman was Helen Bayly, a member of a local League of Women Voters chapter, who became active in the abortion issue after being forced to have two psychiatrists pronounce her mentally unstable in order to obtain an abortion when she became pregnant for the fifth time. "Explaining this to strange men outraged me," Bayly said. " 'I'm going to kill my kids,' I raged. I said I'll go berserk. I felt that way. I felt like a tigress. I felt I was clawing my way out of a thicket."[54] Unlike many women, who even after enduring similar treatment did not want to become politically involved, Bayly became a vocal supporter of abortion reform, testifying at a legislative hearing in Albany in the spring of 1968 and lobbying legislators. Although the League of Women Voters had not taken a position on abortion in the late 1960s, its legislative office in Albany posted lists of local legislators and their positions on abortion. Bayly recalled that she used the political experience she had gained by watching other league members work on such community issues as day care.

Individual women's reasons for contributing time or money to the abortion repeal campaign varied. Some had had illegal abortions or had helped friends obtain them. Others may have been afraid to participate actively, but contributed money. Whatever their reasons, it's fair to say that some women were mobilized by the alternative discourses and story lines created by groups such as the CCS and NOW. In the words of Redstockings cofounder Ellen Willis, the discourse shifted from "What can we do to make them more compassionate?" to "Women have a right to control their freedom, their reproductive rights."[55]

By this time, radical feminists were sufficiently organized to be an added catalyst for change. They held public demonstrations in favor of abortion repeal. A state legislative hearing on abortion reform held in New York in February 1969 was picketed by pro-repealers, some of whom broke into the hearing and claimed that women were the only "real experts" on abortion and demanded to be heard.[56] A month later, some of these women formed the radical feminist group Redstockings and held a mock hearing at the Washington Square Methodist Church in New York City, where women talked about their experiences with illegal abortions.[57]

"The speak-out occurred after the abortion hearing," recalled Irene Peslikis, an early member of Redstockings. "We decided it was absolutely necessary for women to go public about what was really going on. We were getting abortions anyway. Illegally. And risking our lives and being devastated by this experience. . . .

"Redstockings organized a panel. I think it was about 15 women . . . and a church packed full of people who showed up with a vengeance. Everybody was interested in this speak-out. They had never heard of such a thing! . . . I think that our contribution, the radical contribution, was to give a real momentous push. That's what I think we did. I don't think things would have moved like they did without that. . . . Because it was so true and authentic and real. Everybody felt it."[58]

According to Ellen Willis, she and Shulamith Firestone conceived of Redstockings as a militant action group.[59] The organization's demonstrations were intended to be a kind of mass consciousness-raising to convince people that abortion was a political issue as well as a "women's issue," a new concept in the late 1960s.[60] Another radical group, New Yorkers for Abortion Law Repeal, founded by Lucinda Cisler and James Clapp, also staged demonstrations to generate support for repeal. Its members demonstrated in Albany, and they passed out leaflets in favor of repeal at the American Medical Association's 1969 convention in Manhattan.[61]

In the spring of 1969, pro-abortion activists organized the first national conference for abortion repeal. At its conclusion, the National Association for the Repeal of Abortion Laws (NARAL) was established to mobilize activists throughout the country and to coordinate strategies and resources in states where success seemed most likely.[62] By the end of the year, state legislatures in Arkansas, Delaware, New Mexico, and Oregon passed abortion-reform bills. The *Belous* and *Vuitch* cases challenging restrictive abortion laws were handed down. The publicity that these decisions received strengthened the national abortion-repeal movement.

It's unlikely that the courts would have considered abortion to be part of a woman's constitutional right to privacy without the efforts of abortion activists to bring cases challenging the laws. The same can be said for the evolving feminist discourse that defined access to abortion as a woman's reproductive right. As Aryeh Neier observed, "Feminism created a sense of urgency to which all officials of all branches of government responded. . . . A change that seemed unthinkable a few years ago was brought about because the emerging feminist movement had radically changed the political climate."[63]

Lucinda Cisler put it this way:

> At first people who were already in the abortion movement who'd worked on reform were somewhat leery to bring it up—believe it or not—as a woman's issue. . . . They'd say, 'That will scare legislators. . . . ' But what is it, you know? It is a public health issue, it is a doctors' rights issue, it is a population control issue, it is all those other things, but finally it's this damn woman who is pregnant and who doesn't want to be pregnant and she's going to do something about it. . . .
> So pretty soon it became obvious that saying, 'Hey, it's the woman's right,' was a very powerful, American, democratic, libertarian argument that appealed to a lot of people. . . . It was this boldness of saying, 'Hey, it's my right!' plus the already existing abortion movement—as quite distinct from the feminist movement. Without both of those, nothing could have happened. Because women sitting around and talking or demonstrating or even breaking into hearings as feminists alone could not have done it, and this reform movement mousing along without an infusion of feminism couldn't have done much either except pass a bunch more [ALI] laws.[64]

The final blow for activists still tied to the concept of reform was the third defeat of Blumenthal's reform bill in April 1969 by a 78-to-69 vote. After several hours of debate,

Martin Ginsberg, a Republican, delivered a speech in which he drew an analogy between fetal deformity and his own disability from polio: "If we are prepared to say that a life should not come into this world malformed or abnormal, then tomorrow we should be prepared to say that a life already in this world which becomes malformed or abnormal should not be permitted to live. I don't know why God saw fit to let me live in this form and condition. Perhaps it was so I could be here on April 17 to speak on this specific bill."[65]

Ginsberg's speech illustrated the inherent political weakness of the reform position: its ambiguity. This was what enabled opponents to exploit the emotional aspects of the issue and to repeatedly defeat reform bills. Blumenthal, however, remained undeterred, as he continued to see abortion primarily as a public-health issue. Throughout the year, though he met with repeal supporters, he continued to support reform. In November, however, members of New Yorkers for Abortion Law Repeal forced the issue by circulating petitions for repeal in Blumenthal's district on Election Day.[66] Faced with the signatures of several thousand of his constituents, he abandoned the reform position and joined the repealers.

The Vote: 1970

With no more reform bills to contend with, abortion forces were able to go solely for repeal, a tactic that clarified the issue for legislators and their constituents.[67] In January of 1970, Cook and Leichter introduced their second repeal bill. The new bill, unlike the 1969 version, defined abortion as "treatment of a physical condition" that only a licensed physician could legally perform, thus returning it to the criminal code instead of leaving its regulation to the health law.[68] Without the physician requirement, Cook and Leichter risked the opposition of a large segment of the New York medical community, which was grappling with the repeal position while doctors across the country were dividing over abortion reform. Without the physician requirement, Leichter said, "We couldn't have gotten five votes."[69]

While Cook and Leichter saw these conditions as necessary compromises, the radical wing of New Yorkers for Abortion Law Repeal vehemently opposed the criminalization of abortion and the physician requirement because these conditions gave control over abortions to physicians and the government, not to women. They also wanted to make abortions easier to obtain by allowing other medical personnel, such as paramedics, to perform them.

But another faction within NYALR, led by Ruth Proskauer Smith, the former executive director of the Association for the Study of Abortion, agreed with Cook and Leichter that these changes were necessary to get any kind of repeal bill passed, and formed the Cook-Leichter Committee to organize legislative support for the 1970 bill.[70] NARAL endorsed the committee, provided it with seed money, and lent it its mailing list.[71] At its first two meetings, in January and February 1970, the committee elected officers and gathered endorsements from more than fifty organizations whose representatives had been invited to join the repeal coalition.[72]

The Cook-Leichter Committee became the communications center of the repeal network, which until then had not had one. Though this lack of organization lent itself to the kind of spontaneous grassroots mobilization that had characterized the early reform campaign, it would have been unsuitable for the 1970 campaign Cook and Leichter were leading. The repeal position was new to most legislators, and pro-abortion forces had to translate support for reform into support for repeal within a matter of months. They also needed to attract additional support to overtake the NYCC. The committee's strength lay in its ongoing efforts to broaden the statewide coalition and to target undecided legislators.

The Cook-Leichter Committee distributed pamphlets, sent mailings to medical and religious groups, and recruited volunteers throughout the state.[73] To secure legislative support, it used two different strategies, reflecting the different political dynamics of each region. Downstate, it concentrated its efforts on the reform clubs and the news media, which had been the reformers' bases from the start, and on coordinating with local grassroots groups.[74] In Albany it used members of small community and church groups to lobby individual legislators directly, feeling that upstate legislators were more sensitive to their constituents than were downstate legislators, who would vote the way their leaders instructed. "The upstate legislators were infinitely more sensitive," Cook explained. "New York city legislators today [1976], I believe, are more sensitive. But back in 1970 more of them did what they were told to do by their leaders. . . . On the Republican side, we had a few who the boss told how to vote. But I knew those too. And I knew the bosses."[75]

One activist who worked with the committee put it this way: "There was some red-faced bastard that had to be talked to. And I'd go and put a smile on my face—I wouldn't tell him it was my body and I could do what I wanted. I'd talk about how good it was for the children, and that he was off the hook because he wouldn't have to make the decision [if he voted for repeal]."[76]

In February 1970, the Senate leadership decided to hold its floor debate on the bill before the Assembly's debate, concluding that if the bill was passed by the Senate, which was considered to the more conservative chamber, its chances in the Assembly would be improved.[77] The Cook-Leichter Committee was sufficiently organized to send telegrams to all the Senators, urging them to separate their religious beliefs from their votes.[78] This strategy framed access to abortion in terms of rights and liberties, as opposed to the moral arguments against repeal made by the Catholic Conference.[79] It also worked for upstate Republicans, who were "big on freedom of the individual."[80] Clinton Dominick, the chief sponsor of the Senate version of the repeal bill, felt that the usual charges of partisanship and religious affiliation were inappropriate, and he did not lobby his colleagues on these grounds.[81] In March 1970, for the first time, the Senate passed a repeal bill. The vote was 31 to 26.[82]

Repeal forces immediately accelerated their campaign for Assembly votes. To release the bill, the Codes Committee had insisted on two compromises: a parents' consent provision and a twenty-four-week limitation on abortions, except when the woman's life was in danger.[83] The consent requirement was added in response to fears that easier access to abortion might prompt teenagers to get abortions they didn't want, and also that it might lead to black genocide.[84] The time limitation was based on the common-law concept of quickening, which served as a legal precedent for repeal. Cook and her cosponsors agreed to the consent clause, but the time limit proved more difficult for them to accept, because it went against the purpose of repeal, which was to give women the power to decide to terminate a pregnancy. Judging that she would gain several votes by accepting the conditions and lose few, if any, Cook relented.[85]

On March 30, Cook brought the bill to the floor, where hours of speeches and attempts to amend it prolonged the debate into the evening. The vote, when it finally began after midnight, was 73 to 71 against the bill.[86] Cook decided against a second vote, and tabled the bill so that it could be reintroduced. The following week, the NYCC succeeded in persuading three Catholic assemblymen to switch their votes and oppose the bill; one of these was Anthony Stella, a reform Democrat.[87] Concluding that more time would be detrimental to the bill's chances, Cook moved to take the bill from the table, knowing that she had the votes for the next round.

On April 9, the Assembly voted on the repeal bill for a second time, with the vote ending in a 74-to-74 tie. Then, as had been agreed earlier,[88] George Michaels, an upstate Democrat, rose and addressed the speaker: "What's the use of getting elected if you don't stand for something?" Michaels said. "I realize, Mr. Speaker, that I am terminating my political career, but I cannot sit here and allow my vote to be the one that defeats this bill—I ask that my vote be changed from 'no' to 'yes.'"[89]

The first time round, the speaker, Perry Duryea, had been able to prevent a showdown on the bill by neglecting to include votes recorded earlier in the evening by members who had left the floor.[90] On the second vote he was unable to do this, and so voted in favor of the bill, pushing the bill over to a 76-to-73 passage.[91] The following day, the Senate approved the Assembly bill, 31 to 26, and Governor Rockefeller signed it into law on April 11. On July 1, 1970, the most liberal abortion-repeal law in the country went into effect in New York.[92]

"If the vote were to come up today," Constance Cook said in 1976, "we'd lose it resoundingly. Resoundingly. Because since 1970, every candidate, everybody's who's ever said they might think about running, gets their little visitations from anti-abortionists. . . . this is something a politician doesn't want to take on."[93]

Notes

1. Lader 1973, p. vii.
2. *The New York Times*, January 31, 1965, p. 73.
3. Association for the Study of Abortion, Headquarters Report, 1966, p. 1.
4. Lader 1973, p. 12.
5. Ibid. p. 57.
6. Ibid.
7. Neier 1992, p. 114.
8. The bill was passed on to Blumenthal because Percy Sutton, the sponsor of the 1966 abortion-reform bill, had been elected Manhattan borough president and had resigned from the Assembly. Lader 1973, p. 59.
9. Interview, Marsha Aranoff, Blumenthal's legislative assistant, New York City, July 1, 1992.
10. They included the New York Obstetrical Society, the New York County Medical Society, the State Council of Churches, the United Synagogues of America, the New York Civil Liberties Union, and the New York Bar Association's Committee on Public Health (Lader 1973, pp. 58–60).
11. In November of 1965, voters approved a constitutional convention, to be held in 1967. The NYCC began mobilizing support, hoping to repeal the Blaine amendment during the convention. On the Blaine amendment, see Morgan 1968, pp. 109–27. For an analysis of Cardinal Spellman's political influence, see Cooney 1984. On Spellman's active interest in public aid for parochial schools, see Cooney 1984, Ch. 14.
12. For the complete text of the bishops' letter, see *The New York Times*, February 13, 1967, p. A1.
13. Sarat 1982, p. 128.
14. Blumenthal supported the liberalization of divorce laws in New York, which was opposed by the bishops. He also cosponsored a bill that would have made it a felony for law-enforcement officials to wiretap or listen in on private conversations without one party's consent (*The New York Times*, February 13, 1967, pp. A1, A50).

15. Despite reformers' success in defeating some machine candidates within Manhattan, the regulars still held the majority of elected offices in the five boroughs (Shefter p. 102).

16. Howard Moody, telephone interview, February 13, 1992. The following account is based on this interview except where noted.

17. Aryeh Neier interview, New York City, February 10, 1992.

18. These included the American Lutheran Church, New York City's Protestant Council of Churches, and political and charitable organizations such as the Americans for Democratic Action, the American Friends Service Committee, and the State Charities Aid Society (Lader [p. 58]). The New York chapter of the ACLU provided the CCS with free legal counsel from the start (Neier 1992, Carmen and Moody 1973, p. 25), but was not at the forefront of the movement in New York.

19. Before establishing the OALR, Lassoe organized the Abortion Reform Association, which was funded largely by Stuart Mott, a wealthy supporter. One of their main purposes was to run advertisements in *The New York Times* to generate support for abortion reform. Membership in the association was limited to individuals, and Lassoe realized that institutional support was also needed to change the laws, so he created the OALR (John Lassoe interview, New York City, February 12, 1992).

20. Ibid.

21. The OALR was the moving force behind the petition drive for the first Blumenthal bill. See Note 10.

22. Staggenborg makes a similar observation about the early days of the abortion movement (1991, p. 27).

23. Lassoe interview. For the Episcopal Church's position on abortion reform, see the testimony of the Right Reverend George W. Barrett, Episcopal bishop of Rochester (Joint Legislative Committee on Problems of Public Health, Medicare, Medicaid, and Compulsory Health and Hospital Insurance, Rochester, New York, February 20, 1969).

24. Henrik Dullea, former employee of the New York Catholic Conference, interview, Ithaca, N.Y., December 20, 1991.

25. After the 1970 abortion-repeal bill passed in New York, Cardinal Cooke became actively engaged. He later became chairman of the bishops' committee on pro-life affairs.

26. Interview with Dullea.

27. *Family Planning Oral History Project,* p. 69.

28. Edward Golden interview, Troy, N.Y., April 8, 1992.

29. During an interview with Alan Davitt, executive director of the NYCC in the 1960s, one of his colleagues, Kathleen Gallagher, who sat in on the interview, recalled that Tobin had discussed the necessity for lay people such as Golden to recruit non-Catholics to the campaign against

abortion reform. Golden was invited to attend national and regional meetings of the USCC in early 1967 (Interview, Albany, N.Y., April 7, 1992).

30. Shapiro 1972, p. 10.

31. Golden interview.

32. *The New York Times,* April 4, 1968, p. 1.

33. Between 1965 and 1967, four states passed ALI-type laws; between 1968 and 1970, nine other states passed reform laws and four states repealed their laws. The only state to pass an ALI law after 1970 was Florida in 1972. No states repealed their laws after 1971. For the influence of the ALI code on early efforts to reform the laws, see George 1973, p. 18.

34. *Oral History Project,* p. 41.

35. By limited repeal, I mean the elimination of restrictions that affect most women who usually obtain abortions in the first trimester. Outright repeal would eliminate all restrictions on abortions, including time limits and the requirement that only physicians perform them.

36. Radical feminists favored a pure repeal bill that took abortion out of medical and criminal codes and guaranteed women the right to abortion without restriction throughout their pregnancy. The problems this posed for legislators in New York and why they agreed to restrictions are discussed later in this chapter. See Baehr 1990 for the radical feminists' argument.

37. A poll commissioned by the Association for the Study of Abortion in December 1967 found that 75 percent of New York State residents (and 72 percent of Catholics) favored a liberalized abortion law. See *The New York Times,* January 10, 1968, p. A23.

38. At its conclusion, the majority report from the committee recommended the adoption of an ALI-type abortion-reform bill and added a provision for abortions on demand for women with four or more children (Lader 1973, p. 128).

39. Another setback for the NYCC was the final outcome of the Blaine amendment. Although the NYCC succeeded in repealing Blaine as part of the overall constitutional revision in 1967, the constitutional package itself was resoundingly rejected the following year by 3,364,630 votes to 1,309,897. See Morgan 1968, p. 125.

40. Private papers of Dr. Ruth Cusak. Cook was part of the Republican hierarchy and chairwoman of the Education Committee and the Republican Program Committee. She represented the 125th Assembly District in central New York, comprising Tioga and Tompkins Counties.

41. Constance Cook, interview, Ithaca, N.Y., October 31, 1991.

42. *Oral History Project,* p. 45.

43. Cook interview.

44. *Oral History Project,* p. 42.

45. Traina 1975, p. 17.

46. Cusak had a Ph.D. in nutrition, but generally did not use her title because she found that it intimidated people she needed to work with. The following is based on my interview with Ruth Cusak, Miller Place, N.Y., December 2, 1997.

47. *Oral History Project,* p. 34.

48. The following description of the CPL is based on several telephone interviews I had with members of the group in October 1998.

49. Trudy Carpenter, an early member of the CPL, telephone interview, October 24, 1998.

50. *Oral History Project,* pp. 51–52.

51. These included the YMCA, Planned Parenthood, the CCS, the Schenectady Inner City Mission, the Council of the Community Services of Albany, and the Schenectady Community Action Program.

52. Private papers of Lawrence Lader, Rare Books and Manuscript Division, New York Public Library.

53. Mary Freeman, interview, editor of the CPL's newsletter, October 25, 1998.

54. Helen Bayly, interview, New York City, January 2, 1998.

55. Ellen Willis, interview, Brooklyn, N.Y., April 11, 1992.

56. Hole and Levine 1971, p. 296.

57. For a vivid description of the mock hearing, see Baehr 1990, pp. 41–42.

58. Ibid.

59. Willis interview.

60. Ibid.

61. New Yorkers for Abortion Law Repeal newsletters, April 2, 1969, and June 13, 1969, Schlesinger Library.

62. Lader 1973, p. 89.

63. Neier 1992, p. 118.

64. Quoted in Baehr 1990, p. 43.

65. *The New York Times,* April 18, 1969, p. 1.

66. Lader 1973, pp. 129–30.

67. This view was supported by Clinton Dominick, a Republican from Newburgh, the sponsor of the Senate version of the repeal bill. He maintained that abortion repeal was preferable to abortion reform because it was simpler and therefore easier to debate. Interview with Dominick, Newburgh, New York, March 27, 1992.

68. Cook didn't think this difference was significant because the outcome would be the same: Either the health code or the penal code would

require that abortions be done by a licensed physician (*Oral History Project,* p. 58).

69. Quoted in Lader 1973, p. 130. Both changes increased the control of physicians and the state, and silenced fears that elective abortions would be unregulated and would become a public-health disaster.

70. Ibid.

71. Ibid.

72. *Chronicle of the Activities of the Committee for the Cook-Leichter Bill* (May 1970, p. 1). Private papers of Ruth Proskauer Smith. Used with permission.

73. Ibid.

74. The committee also worked with local organizations in several downstate districts that organized letter-writing campaigns in favor of the repeal bill. One of these was the Suffolk Committee for Abortion Law Repeal, established by Ruth Cusak, which contacted community organizations and asked them to send letters to legislators (*Chronicle of the Cook-Leichter Bill,* p. 2). Another was the Nassau Committee for Abortion Law Repeal that was helped in the beginning by its sister organization in Suffolk County. Members of the Nassau committee persuaded Assemblyman Martin Ginsberg, whose 1968 speech on the floor was credited with defeating the abortion reform bill of that year, to join with other Republicans as a sponsor of the 1970 repeal bill. They convinced him that by switching his vote, he could rehabilitate his reputation with moderate and liberal Republicans who supported repeal.

75. *Oral History Project* (p. 54). This interpretation was confirmed by Senators Dominick and Leichter in interviews I had with them.

76. This quote is taken from an interview with an activist who requested anonymity.

77. Richard Perez-Pena, " '70 Abortion Law: New York said Yes, Stunning the Nation," *The New York Times,* April 9, 2000, pp. 1 and 27.

78. Lader 1973, p. 133.

79. Senator Leichter recalled that a number of legislators who had voted against Blumenthal's reform bills felt they could vote in favor of repeal on libertarian grounds (interview with Leichter by author). In addition, some Catholic legislators who supported repeal, such as Edward Speno, a Nassau County Republican, felt that by voting to repeal Blaine, they had met their commitment to their Catholic constituency and could vote for repeal if their other constituents favored it (Lader 1973, p. 128).

80. One example is that of Paul Bookson, an Orthodox Jew who had a large number of reform Democrats in his district. Bookson voted for repeal, allegedly after he was threatened with defeat by other reformers (ibid., p. 134).

81. This was more true in the Senate than in the Assembly, where battle lines from past attempts to pass the Blumenthal bill had been drawn (Dominick interview).

82. Eighteen Democrats and thirteen Republicans voted in favor of the bill. Seven of the eighteen Democrats were reformers. See chart, Chapter Six.

83. Lader 1973, p. 136.

84. Ibid.

85. *Oral History Project,* p. 73.

86. The "yes" votes of two legislators who had left the hall were not counted by Duryea in the final tally (though they had been recorded by the teller). This legislative practice, though legal, is seldom used (Lader 1973, pp. 138–39]).

87. The other two were Joseph Lisa and Hulan Jack (ibid. p. 142).

88. Although Michaels' switch was described as a "surprise" by the press, Cook maintained that Michaels, who represented a large Catholic constituency, had agreed to switch if his vote was needed, though Cook would try to avoid this, as she knew it would cost him his career. Cook had a similar conversation with Duryea, who agreed to vote in favor of the bill in the event of a tie (*Oral History Project,* pp. 29–30). Cook confirmed this in my interview with her.

89. Michael's speech quoted in Lader 1973, p. 143.

90. See Note 86.

91. For a partisan breakdown of the vote, see Chapter Six.

92. For an analysis of the unsuccessful attempt to reverse the 1970 Abortion Repeal Bill, see Lader 1973, Chapter 14.

93. *Oral History Project,* p. 78.

5 Interest-Group Politics in Pennsylvania

In the midst of a nationwide effort to update abortion statutes, the one state that went against the tide was Pennsylvania. Beginning in 1967, the Pennsylvania Catholic Conference (PCC) built a well-organized, comprehensive campaign on the state and local levels that pre-empted its opponents and generated broad-based legislative support for restrictive abortion policy.

Several factors contributed to the triumph of antiabortion forces in Pennsylvania. Chief among them was the reformers' lack of interest in taking control of the Democratic Party machine in the 1950s. As a result, the party was closed to new-interest, including pro-abortion, activists in the following decade. This enabled the PCC to strengthen its alliance on reproductive issues with the party and to promote an antiabortion discourse with little interference. As in New York, the relevant events unfolded in two stages. The dates of the stages do not exactly correspond, however, because the Pennsylvania campaign started two years later than the one in New York.

The First Stage: 1965–1969

Abortion Reform

In 1967, William Scranton's lieutenant governor, Raymond Shafer, succeeded him as governor. The following year, Shafer fulfilled a campaign pledge by calling a constitutional convention.[1] During the 1967 legislative session, a series of reform bills were introduced to update the state's constitution. One of these, Senate Bill 38,[2] was written to clarify Pennsylvania's abortion statute, which prohibited unlawful abortions but did not describe the difference between legal and illegal ones.[3] Section 1803 of the bill was an attempt to update the abortion laws in Pennsylvania according to the guidelines established by the American Law Institute.

In this first stage, strong party support was essential if an abortion-reform bill was to get out of committee and onto the floor. So, too, was the creation of a pro-abortion discourse coalition to counter the antiabortion discourse being established by the PCC. Neither of these developments occurred. One reason was the the approach to reform adopted by pro-abortion forces; another was the Democratic Party's alliance with the PCC on reproductive issues, which pre-dated the abortion debate.

In 1965, the Office of Public Assistance recommended allowing its staff to discuss contraception with poor families that continued to have children.[4] The recommendation was opposed by Archbishop Krol of Philadelphia, who released the following statement on behalf of all the Catholic bishops in the state:

> The action now contemplated by the Department of Public
> Welfare launches Pennsylvania upon a dangerous experiment
> with the lives of the poor. The poor have not sought this

program. Others have sought it for them. The Catholic Church through centuries has manifested its love for those afflicted with poverty. Monuments to that love may be seen in the form of Catholic Welfare Agencies. . . .

While the department justifies the program mainly in terms of providing public assistance recipients with 'opportunities for medical care,' it is commonly known that the main groups pressuring for government birth control have far broader aims, such as involving the state in what the department calls 'family functioning,' or exerting control over families in order to limit population growth. . . . These activities are not the business of the state, and they are serious threats to civil liberty.[5]

Martin Mullen, the Democratic chairman of the House Appropriations Committee, and William Ball, general counsel to the PCC, worked together to reverse the directive. Mullen introduced a rider on the appropriations bill, stipulating that birth-control programs not be funded by public monies. Later, at the bill's hearing, Mullen and William Ball, general council for the PCC, testified against the directive issued by the Office of Public Assistance. In Harrisburg, Ball established an ad hoc committee to organize a public campaign against the recommendation. The campaign included a full-page ad, signed by all the bishops in Pennsylvania, that appeared in more than fifty Pennsylvania newspapers. In addition, a pamphlet entitled *Betty and Jack Talk About Government Birth Control* was distributed, and sermons against birth control were given during Sunday services.[6]

The alliance between the Democratic Party and the PCC on birth control was expanded two years later to include the issue of abortion-law reform. Since there was minimal organized support for abortion reform in Pennsylvania in 1967, SB 38 had little chance of passing.[7] Nonetheless, within a month of the bill's introduction, the PCC drafted the following statement: "Abortion is the willful destruction of a human being. The proponents of the proposed legislation take the position that destruction of innocent human life is justified in response to certain social or personal ills. This position is totally repugnant to the traditional view of American and Pennsylvania law, that human life is sacred. . . ."

The PCC's antiabortion discourse also sought to cast abortion-reform supporters as dishonest and morally suspect. "It is greatly to be feared that the certification of abortion, on the ground of danger to 'mental health,' would in a short time lead to so-called 'abortion on demand.' Any unmarried woman could very easily substantiate an impairment to her 'mental health.' If she could not substantiate an impairment to her mental health she would need only to make a passionate cry of 'Rape!' and she would be entitled to an abortion. If she were under the age of 16 her intercourse, per se illicit, would entitle her to an abortion."[8]

From the start, the PCC waged a meticulous legislative campaign against abortion reform. William Ball wrote to Governor-elect Raymond Shafer in January of 1967 to reiterate the conference's opposition to abortion reform, and to request that Shafer honor his pledge to oppose it, a pledge he had made at a meeting with the PCC in October 1966.[9] Ball got in touch with several legislators, requesting support in defeating any attempts to reform the laws, and several hundred "lay contacts," whom he kept informed of the PCC's strategy on abortion reform.[10]

After SB 38 died in committee in 1967, the PCC continued organizing. In 1968 it established an Ad Hoc Committee on Abortion, based on the guidelines suggested by the Family Bureau of the United States Catholic Conference, and appointed "right-to-life coordinators" in each of the state's eight dioceses to facilitate efforts to prevent any future changes in the abortion statute. The bureau's program called for the active participation of the state conferences, the establishment of a Right-to Life Committee within each diocese, and the creation of a group to foster non-Catholic support for restrictive abortion legislation.[11]

The PCC's general assumption was that a pro-abortion campaign would eventually come to Pennsylvania, as it had to other states, including neighboring New York. The group's strategy was twofold: to move swiftly and consistently to kill reform bills in committee before public hearings could be held, and to build broad-based support for restrictive abortion policy.[12] By defining abortion as murder, and by suggesting that its supporters were morally flawed or sexually promiscuous, the PCC used a religious discourse to discredit abortion reform and its supporters.

Grassroots Support for Reform

The first sign of organized support for abortion reform came in April 1967, when the Pennsylvania Council of Churches prepared a position paper in support of SB 38. Declaring that "No one person or group has possession of the truth," the council defined abortion as an issue of individual freedom.[13] The following year, since no reform coalition existed in this period, the council turned its attention to providing abortion counseling, with the creation of a Philadelphia chapter of the Clergy Consultation Service (CCS).

In 1968, a small group of women approached several clergymen and asked them to open an abortion-counseling service. According to Allen Hinand, a Baptist minister who was at the meeting, the group felt that the clergy had the legal immunity needed to establish a service of this kind.[14]

Two of these women, Marilou Theunissen and Barbara McNeel, had spoken with Howard Moody and Arlene Carmen, the founders of the CCS, and McNeel had attended one of the CCS's organizational meetings in New York.[15] In November of 1968, the group elected Hinand to organize the first CCS chapter in Philadelphia.

Unlike its counterpart in New York, the Philadelphia chapter was conceived as a direct service organization rather than a political one.[16] From the start it was an underground operation, with calls being taken by an answering machine.[17] Initially, all the counselors were male clergy; Theunissen conducted training sessions to raise their consciousness about women's reproductive rights.[18] Another of these early chapters was established in Harrisburg, run by the Reverend Paul Gehris. Like Moody and Hinand, Gehris had been involved in the civil-rights movement. He was also influenced by the women's movement and its claim that women had the right to decide how to handle an unwanted pregnancy.[19] He was committed to the idea that the clergy had to be on the cutting edge of social issues if they were to be useful to the community. Gehris recalled that although some of his parishioners were concerned that he was providing abortion counseling in the basement of the church, he had the general support of the Church hierarchy both locally and on the state level.

In this same period, three pro-abortion grassroots groups emerged. In late 1968 Barbara McNeel and Conni Bille organized the Abortion Rights Association, a feminist organization dedicated to mobilizing support for women's rights, specifically reproductive rights.[20] In the first few years, its members spent most of their time giving lectures to community and church groups, writing newsletters, and issuing press releases. The Abortion Justice Association was founded by Patricia Miller to mobilize legislative support for reform. Miller had moved to Pittsburgh from Colorado, where she had been active in the successful abortion-reform movement. In 1969 she organized Pennsylvanians for Choice, an offshoot of the AJA, to organize support across the state for abortion reform.[21] The Pennsylvania Abortion Rights Association (PARA), which was started in 1970 by Phylliss Ryan, concentrated on challenging the Pennsylvania abortion law, training speakers to address community groups on the need to repeal the law, and staging public demonstrations.[22]

As in New York, there was a considerable amount of overlap among the early groups. Several members of PARA worked with the CCS in Philadelphia, and the organizations cooperated by sharing mailing lists and sending members to each other's demonstrations. Later, some members of the CCS and PARA founded Concern for Health Options: Information, Care and Education (CHOICE) to provide abortion referrals and other health-care services for women. None of these groups was politically coordinated until 1972, however—five years after SB 38 had been introduced. There were several reasons for this.

First was the civic, as opposed to political, nature of reform in Philadelphia, which had characterized reform movements in the city since the nineteenth century.[23] The advocacy approach to abortion rights in Pennsylvania was manifested more in the promotion of direct services than through legislative mobilization. Given the dire necessity of providing women with access to safe abortions, this was understandable, but it was not politically efficacious. The Philadelphia chapters of the National Organization for Women and the National Women's Political Caucus, which were not formed until the early 1970s, shared this approach toward abortion policy, with the majority of their members working toward the passage of the equal-rights amendment, not on changing the abortion laws.[24]

Second was the vagueness of the Pennsylvania abortion statute itself. Arlen Specter, the Philadelphia district attorney during this period, interpreted illegal abortions to be those done by unlicensed individuals in private homes or offices, and his office did not prosecute physicians who were performing therapeutic abortions. In some quarters of the activist community the feeling was that it was better to leave the law unchallenged, so women who needed abortions could get them in Philadelphia or Pittsburgh rather than being compelled to go to New York.

The third reason was the absence of party support. With no abortion-reform bills being introduced and no coalition of interest groups pressing for change, there was no rallying point around which pro-abortion forces could organize. This lack of political coordination allowed the PCC to shape the legislative agenda and to dominate the public discourse on abortion policy in this first stage. Unlike the pro-abortion activists, the PCC had a clear political strategy in place. It was well organized, had access to the Democratic Party, and could draw on a statewide network of churches and diocesan offices capable of mobilizing support for its activities. In addition, the PCC's position on abortion reform was supported by its earlier campaign against birth control and by Vatican II's statement opposing abortion. By 1970, the PCC had established itself as the leading organization on abortion policy in the state; pro-abortion activists were only beginning to mobilize.

The Second Stage: 1970–1972

The main activity of both sides during the second stage of the abortion battle was centered on grassroots and legislative mobilization. The chief goal was to define abortion in terms that would mobilize public support for their respective positions. The PCC, which had been expecting another reform bill since 1967, expanded its efforts on the local level with the formation of Pennsylvanians for Human Life (PHL), and by working with right-to-life coordinators in each diocese.[25] Pro-abortion activists sought to widen the scope of the debate with the establishment of the Governor's Commission on Abortion and the introduction of a reform bill in 1970, which was followed by a repeal bill in 1971.

Grassroots Mobilization

The PCC's strategy in this stage was twofold: to remain on the defensive as long as possible, and to be prepared to go on the offensive when necessary. It continued working to create a consistent antiabortion policy across the state that would be supported by the dioceses and would lay the groundwork for the anticipated legislative battle. In 1969 it established the PHL, the first statewide antiabortion group, to increase support for restrictive abortion laws. In the following year it organized regional chapters of the PHL throughout the state. Each chapter was coordinated by a priest and managed by a steering committee. Chapters were responsible for recruiting members, for community outreach and education, and for making contacts with the local news media. In addition, committees were established to coordinate letter-writing campaigns to legislators and to sponsor meetings with local representatives.[26]

Like the Catholic hierarchy on the national level, the PCC realized that to create majority support to defeat repeal and reform laws, it would have to mobilize people outside the Church.[27] It began to recruit non-Catholics to join PHL chapters; as a result, the PHL increasingly contained members who favored abortion in cases of incest and rape—a position adamantly opposed by the official Catholic position. According to Jane Arnold, president of the southeastern region of the PHL, many Catholic members thought that these exceptions were necessary to retain public support for restrictive laws.[28] In 1971, to counteract this divergence from the Church's position, the PCC gave its right-to-life coordinators the responsibility for organizing Catholic right-to-life programs in each diocese alongside the PHL chapters.

Meanwhile, the PHL chapters and the dioceses continued to work together. The relationship was a symbiotic one: The PCC needed the grassroots support that the PHL could provide, and the PHL needed the organizational resources of the Catholic Church.[29] Jane Arnold recalled that the PHL was allowed to distribute its newsletters on "Human Life Sundays," which the Pennsylvania Dioceses held intermittently throughout the year. "All you would have to do was to contact the pastors to distribute literature, to put a note in the bulletin. . . . It [the Church] had the structure to disseminate your information. [You] could work through the Church structure . . . which had 360 parishes."[30] By 1970 the PCC's antiabortion campaign had three levels: a legislative strategy coordinated in Harrisburg, a diocesan campaign that organized churchgoers and groups interested in the issue, and a statewide grassroots movement that generated public support for restrictive abortion policy.

As the PHL was expanding, the first nonsectarian antiabortion grassroots group was founded by Mary Winter, president of the Pittsburgh chapter of the La Leche League. Winter established Women Concerned for the Unborn Child (WCUC), which became one of the largest grassroots antiabortion organizations in the state. From its inception, it was conceived as an organization for women opposed to changes in the abortion law. "It was a spontaneous uprising of Christian women who were horrified. All of us were mothers. At our first formal meeting we took up a collection of what people had in their purses. Our first treasury had twelve dollars, and we went to buy stamps, a church lent us a mimeograph, we made a mailing to everyone we knew, and it just grew, and grew, and grew."[31]

In 1970, the WCUC had a membership of 800.[32] As with other small antiabortion groups, the WCUC's most valuable resource was the commitment of its members, who spoke to community groups, participated in local debates, picketed the local chapter of Planned Parenthood, and baked cookies for a community bazaar.[33] Members also maintained a letter-writing campaign to legislators, and later went to Harrisburg for several antiabortion demonstrations.

According to Winter, the Pittsburgh diocese approached the WCUC and attempted to bring it into closer contact with its right-to-life coordinator.[34] The WCUC resisted, its leaders concluding that to attract broad-based support, it was essential to remain nonsectarian. The group did, however, work with the PHL in contacting candidates running for county office and in participating in various community activities and demonstrations, including cosponsoring an annual "Celebrate Life" interfaith service.[35]

While antiabortion groups were organizing, pro-abortion activists were stepping up their campaign as well. The passage of New York's repeal bill in the spring of 1970 convinced them that repeal was an imminent reality. "The New York bill showed us it could happen," said Sylvia Stengle, founder of the Lehigh Valley Abortion Rights Association.[36]

Soon afterward, the AJA's Pat Miller contacted Gerald Kaufman, a freshman Democratic assemblyman from Pittsburgh, and asked him to sponsor an abortion-reform bill. Like the abortion activists, Kaufman was influenced by the success of the recently passed repeal bill in New York, but he had intended to wait to see how it worked before introducing a similar bill in Pennsylvania.[37]

At Miller's urging, however, Kaufman agreed to sponsor HB 2393, which would have made therapeutic abortions legal. In exchange, the AJA answered constituents' mail on abortion reform and organized support for the bill.[38] The vagueness of the Pennsylvania abortion statute meant that abortions were being performed in some areas of the state but not in others. HB 2393 would have protected all physicians performing therapeutic abortions in Pennsylvania from criminal prosecution, and would have allowed women needing a therapeutic abortion anywhere in the state to get one. Although Kaufman was doubtful that the bill would pass, he wanted to get the dialogue started.

As expected, the bill was killed in the Judiciary Committee, but the aim of starting a dialogue was realized. In an effort to broaden his appeal among liberals in both parties, Milton Shapp, the Democratic gubernatorial candidate, included abortion reform as part of his platform; his opponent, Lieutenant Governor Broderick, opposed it.[39] Following Kaufman's bill several more abortion bills were introduced in the 1970–71 legislative session, including an ALI-type abortion-reform bill and a bill limiting the funding of abortions for poor women,[40] but the most important of these bills were HB 536, the first abortion-repeal bill introduced in Pennsylvania, and HB 800, the first anti-abortion bill introduced in Pennsylvania, which prohibited all abortions.

Whereas Kaufman's 1970 bill had sought primarily to legalize therapeutic abortions, his 1971 repeal bill, HB 536, defined abortion as a woman's right and was aimed at repealing laws restricting women's access to it in the first trimester.[41] Pro-abortion activists in Pennsylvania recognized the strength of the repeal discourse, just as their New York counterparts had: It eliminated the ambiguity of the reform position and simplified the issues, both for legislators and the public. "It is becoming apparent that legislators have an easier time coping with 'repeal' than with 'reform.' When they try to grapple with the concept of 'justifiable abortion,' they find that as a medical matter it is outside their field of competence, and as a personal moral decision it is outside their authority."[42]

The advantage of simplifying the issue was not lost on the antiabortion forces either. They answered their opponents with the introduction of HB 800, which sought to outlaw all abortions. The bill's preamble, which embraced the premise of the sanctity of life, was similar in tone to the PCC's statement against SB 38 five years earlier:[43] "The Commonwealth of Pennsylvania hereby reaffirms its immemorial recognition that all human life is inviolable regardless of its age or form, whether possessed by the aged, the physically or mentally ill, the handicapped, or the unborn in the womb; that the eroding of the personhood and right to life of any of these will inevitably endanger the enjoyment of the right to life of all of them; and that the Commonwealth continues to have the right to use the force of law for the protection of all human life."[44]

With HB 800, the PCC established its opposition to all abortions, not just to the limited reform proposed by SB 38. The bill was consistent with the position taken by Vatican II, and with the PCC's previous stand on reproductive issues—

that the state should not interfere with conception. With the introduction of HB 536 and HB 800 the battle lines were drawn.

The Governor's Commission

In response to both bills, Governor Milton Shapp announced the establishment of the Pennsylvania Abortion Law Commission in December 1971 to study the issue and to recommend changes in the law. Although grassroots groups claimed credit for the formation of the commission, it's more likely that the main impetus behind Shapp's decision was a desire to divert attention from his controversial pro-abortion position by deferring to the commission's recommendations, a tactic also employed by Governor Rockefeller in New York.[45]

Nevertheless, from a political standpoint the establishment of the commission was a major victory for pro-abortion activists. It lent legitimacy to the issue of reform and its supporters, an especially significant point given the PCC's ongoing campaign to discredit them.[46] Equally important were the public hearings held by the commission, the first ever in Pennsylvania. In addition to the publicity the hearings attracted, they also brought together pro-abortion activists from across the state.[47] In February 1972, before the hearings began, the Association for the Study of Abortion released a public-opinion poll showing that 57 percent of the people surveyed favored abortion reform that would permit a woman to have an abortion in a hospital if she and her doctor agreed it should be done. Thirty-six percent of the people opposed any changes in the law, and 7 percent were undecided.[48]

The PCC expected the commission to support Shapp and recommend that the abortion laws be either reformed or repealed.[49] To discourage this, it recruited people through its right-to-life coordinators to testify at the hearings, and it organized the attendance of antiabortion supporters.[50] Ministers and rabbis were also contacted by the coordinators in an attempt to broaden religious opposition. The WCUC urged its members to contact their legislators to oppose the Kaufman abortion-repeal bill and to support HB 800.[51] The PCC also made plans to issue a minority report in the event that the commission favored changes in the abortion law.

Pro-abortion activists also lined up supporters, including such notables as New York Law School professor Cyril Means and birth control expert Dr. Alan Guttmacher, and clergy members and social workers affiliated with the CCS in Pennsylvania. Although antiabortion forces felt that the commission was stacked against them, Elizabeth Shipley, a member of the commission, recalled that at the beginning of the hearings their positions were evenly distributed.[52] She noted, however, that the repeal of the New York law had influenced the commission's decision: "New York made it feasible for us to make a recommendation that was quite liberal, given Pennsylvania's [religious] composition, with the [Catholic] Conference being very, very strong."[53]

In June 1972, the commission came out not just in favor of reform, but in favor of repeal.[54] The decision provided the catalyst antiabortion forces needed to get HB 800 released from the House Committee on Health and Welfare, where it had remained for more than a year.[55] Antiabortion forces portrayed HB 800 as a response to the report by the Abortion Law Commission, though in fact it had been introduced a year before the report was issued. With the discharge of HB 800, the PCC went on the offensive.

HB 800

Despite the commission's report, HB 536, the first repeal bill introduced in Pennsylvania, was defeated by a large margin—185 to 14—and the House moved on to HB 800. During an emotional and rancorous debate on the floor, legislators on both sides of the aisle sponsored several amendments to HB 800, including some that would have allowed abortions in cases of rape and incest. All of them were defeated by large margins,[56] prompting representative Donald Fox (R) to speak out against both bills. "I opposed House Bill 536 because I do not believe in abortion on demand," Fox told the House, "and I do not believe in abortions as method of birth or population control. But I oppose also House bill 800 today because I feel this bill is too rigid, too lacking in compassion for the persons concerned."[57]

By 112 to 87, the House amended the bill to allow abortions in cases of danger to the woman's life, and the final bill was approved 157 to 34 before the summer recess.[58]

The Senate did not take up the bill until after the November 1972 elections.[59] As Senator Frederick Hobbs (R) recalled, "No one wanted to vote on abortion because it was a no-win situation." The delay let members avoid the electoral consequences of supporting reform measures that were opposed by the PCC but in line with public opinion in Pennsylvania. Rape and incest provisions for therapeutic abortions initially passed in the Senate, 24 to 23, but they were later dropped after strong pressure from antiabortion legislators in the House who were aligned with the PCC.[60] The Senate also took issue with the spousal and parental-consent provisions, which were deleted, and the bill was passed 39 to 9.

Two weeks after the Senate vote, Governor Shapp vetoed HB 800, stating that it was an unduly restrictive bill that endangered the health of women because it did not allow for abortions in the cases of rape or incest, or when the woman's mental or physical health was threatened.[61] Shapp also concluded that the bill contained several provisions that would be held unconstitutional by the courts. An attempt to override Shapp's veto failed, 102 to 76, with twenty-four legislators abstaining. The vote reflected legislators' reluctance to take on Governor Shapp in his first term, and their general disinclination to get involved with an issue that could derail their political futures. In any event, since the veto had been expected, it's difficult to ascertain where many legislators actually stood on abortion policy.[62]

Antiabortion forces considered HB 800 a dry run for future campaigns. Pro-abortion forces realized that although the governor's veto had prevented HB 800 from becoming law, its necessity demonstrated that they were not sufficiently organized, either to defeat the PCC or to pass any type of abortion-reform or -repeal legislation. The pro-abortion mobilization that had begun during the commission's hearings was cut short, however. Two months after Governor Shapp vetoed HB 800, the Supreme Court ruled in *Roe v. Wade* that women had the constitutional right to an abortion in the first trimester of pregnancy with few restrictions. In January 1973, it seemed that the pro-abortion forces had won.

Notes

1. Ted Robb, Shafer's legislative assistant, recalled that at the beginning of his term Shafer had high hopes that constitutional reform would be one of his lasting political accomplishments. Shafer's administration, however, was plagued by fiscal problems that detracted from the reforms his administration implemented (telephone interview with Ted Robb, January 5, 1993).

2. According to William Woodside, Chief Counsel to the Senate from 1965 to 1971, SB 38 was part of a larger reform effort aimed at streamlining the Pennsylvania Constitution. Various reform measures drawn up by the American Bar Association and other organizations were submitted to several of the bipartisan committees working on constitutional reform. Section 1803 of SB 38 was one of these provisions (telephone interview with Woodside, January 19, 1993).

3. The 1939 act prohibited all illegal abortions in Pennsylvania but failed to define an illegal abortion. In *Commonwealth v. Page,* 54 D.&C. 2d 12 (1970), the Center County Court of Common Pleas ruled that the statute was unconstitutional because it failed to meet the requirements of due process.

4. This section on the PCC's involvement in the birth-control issue is based on Dienes 1972, pp. 277–80.

5. "Krol says Birth Control is not State's Business," *Evening Bulletin* (Pittsburgh, Pa.), December 17, 1965, p. 1.

6. Dienes 1972, pp. 277–80. See also Littlewood 1977, pp. 42–43.

7. It's interesting to compare the Pennsylvania case with the Georgia case discussed in Chapter Two. In each state, the initial abortion-reform bill was introduced as part of a broader effort to revise the state's constitution. Whereas this helped Georgia pro-abortion activists to place the issue in the legal framework of constitutional revisions, in Pennsylvania they were preempted by the PCC.

8. Draft Statement of the Pennsylvania Catholic Conference position on Senate Bill 38 (February 20, 1967, pp. 2–3, files of the PCC).

9. William Ball to Governor-elect Shafer, letter dated January 16, 1967 (files of the PCC).

10. The PCC's early strategy on abortion reform was outlined in a memorandum by William Ball, dated February 21, 1967 (files of the PCC).

11. United States Catholic Conference, *Annual Report,* 1967, p. 42.

12. See Note 10.

13. See "Churches Affirm Stand on Abortion," *The Morning Call* (Allentown, Pa.), October 7, 1970.

14. The Reverend Alan Hinand, telephone interview, January 5, 1993.

15. Barbara McNeel Moran, telephone interview, January 11, 1993.

16. See the following discussion on pp. 112–13.

17. In Harrisburg, women calling the CCS chapter heard the following message: "This is the Pennsylvania Consultation Service on Abortion. If you are not a resident of Pennsylvania call. . . . You are being answered electronically and need only take down the number of one of the

following clergymen. When you call tell either the clergyman or his secretary you wish to make an appointment concerning a problem pregnancy" ("A Pregnant Woman's Guide to Harrisburg," April 15, 1970: 3. Harrisburg Area Women's Rights Movement, Private Papers of Pat Greenwald, an early member of CCS-Harrisburg; used with permission).

18. One of the main reasons Marilou Theunissen became involved with the CCS was her participation in the women's movement, which convinced her that women should have a choice about bearing children. She recalled the "litmus test" question she asked members of the clergy: "A woman becomes pregnant before embarking on a trip with her husband and she wants an abortion because her pregnancy is an inconvenience. What would be your response?" (telephone interview with Theunissen, January 17, 1993).

19. The Reverend Paul Gehris, interview, Harrisburg, Pa., July 10, 1992.

20. Moran interview.

21. Pat Miller, interview, Pittsburgh, Pa., October 20, 1992. Letter from Pat Miller to ARA members, February 14, 1970, papers of Pat Miller.

22. On PARA, See *News From PARA,* November 1970.

23. See Chapter One.

24. The first Pennsylvania chapter of NOW was established in Philadelphia in 1970. The following year, the Pennsylvania chapter of the Women's Political Caucus (PWPC-PA) was founded. Although NOW established an abortion referral service in 1971, both groups spent most of their time on consciousness-raising and building support for ratification of the equal-rights amendment. Interview with Jean Ferson, president of NOW-Philadelphia from 1971 to 1973, in Philadelphia, July 13, 1992. Interview with Ernest Ballard, early member of NOW-Philadelphia and PWPC-PA, Philadelphia, July 14, 1992.

25. These were the dioceses of Allentown, Altoona, Erie, Greensburg, Harrisburg, Philadelphia, Pittsburgh, and Scranton.

26. Thomas Noone, president of PHL, interview, Uniontown, Pa., October 21, 1992.

27. United States Catholic Conference, *Annual Report,* 1968, p. 66. The Catholic hierarchy also considered groups such as the PHL and the National Right to Life Committee to be helpful in countering the impression that opposition to abortion existed solely among Catholics.

28. They also thought that because the number of abortions performed in these instances was small, the amount of support these provisions would generate outweighed the Church's opposition (telephone interview with Jane Arnold, Wyncote, Pa., January 27, 1993).

29. Ibid.

30. Ibid.

31. Hickling 1978, p. 10.

32. Women Concerned for the Unborn Child, newsletter, Vol. 1, No. 3 (March 1971).

33. Ibid. WCUC newsletter, Vol. 1, No. 4 (May 1971). The WCUC's activities were similar to those Luker (1984) found among grassroots groups in California. See Ch. 9.

34. Winter concluded that the dioceses assumed that the WCUC would need help to continue their work (interview with Mary Winter, Pittsburgh, October 21, 1992).

35. Women Concerned for the Unborn Child, newsletters, Vol. 1, Nos. 3 and 4 (March 1971 and May 1971).

36. Interview with Sylvia Stengle, Bethlehem, Pa., July 15, 1992.

37. Gerald Kaufman, telephone interview, November 2, 1992.

38. Pennsylvanians in Support of House Bill 2393, organized by Miller, concentrated its attention on building legislative support by coordinating letter-writing and petition campaigns to demonstrate constituents' support for reform. It also called for the establishment of a commission to study abortion reform.

39. Black 1970, p. 1.

40. These included House Bill 749, which would have prohibited advertising for abortion services; House Bill 1959, designed to stop public funding of therapeutic abortions for poor women; Senate Bill 617, an ALI-based bill; and Senate Bill 928, which would have removed abortion from the criminal code (Halva-Neubauer 1992, pp. 263–64).

41. In addition to the routine requirement that abortions be performed by a licensed physician in an accredited hospital or medical facility, HB 536 contained two other restrictions: a sixteen-week time limit for requesting an abortion, and a "conscience clause," which provided that hospitals or physicians opposed to abortion could choose not to perform them.

42. Pennsylvanians In Support of House Bill 536, newsletter (1971, p. 2. Schlesinger Library.

43. See Note 9.

44. The preamble was dropped in the final version of the bill.

45. This interpretation of Shapp's motivation is that of his special assistant, Richard Durand (telephone interview with Durand, December 16, 1992).

46. Three of the fifteen members named to the commission were affiliated with pro-abortion grassroots groups. These were Pat Miller of the AJA, Marilou Theunissen from the CCS, and Elizabeth Shipley from PARA.

47. Pro-abortion activists across Pennsylvania told me that there was a general lack of awareness of the activities of groups in other parts of the state. According to Pat Miller, it was not until the hearings of the Pennsylvania Abortion Law Commission in 1972 that organizations and activists began connecting (interview with Pat Miller, Pittsburgh, Pa., October 20, 1992).

48. Walsh 1972. The poll was conducted by the Oliver Quayle Company.

49. Notes from the Right-To-Life Coordinators' Meeting, February 10, 1972 (files of the PCC).

50. Ibid.

51. WCUC newsletter, Vol. 1, No. 4 (May 1971, p. 1).

52. These opposing opinions were voiced by Howard Fetterhoff, director of the PCC's Harrisburg chapter, in an interview on July 9, 1992, and by Elizabeth Shipley in an interview in Narbeth, PA, on July 15, 1992.

53. Interview with Shipley.

54. See *Pennsylvania Abortion Law Commission Majority Report*, June 1972: 3–7. Several members of the commission refused to sign the majority's recommendations and submitted their own. See *Pennsylvania Abortion Law Commission Minority Report*, June 1972: 84–96. The minority report echoed the sentiment of the PCC that the commission had been stacked against pro-life supporters (ibid., pp. 75–81).

55. Mullen pressured the committee to release HB 800 by threatening to file a discharge resolution. See "State House Unit Clears 2 Bills on Abortion—One Pro, One Con," *The Philadelphia Inquirer*, June 15, 1972, p. 4.

56. The referendum was rejected 143 to 54; provisions for rape and incest were rejected 127 to 68 and 134 to 63 respectively. See Brutto 1972a.

57. Quote from Representative Donald Fox, *Legislative Journal-House*, June 22, 1972: 3230.

58. See "Liberalized Bill on Abortion Fails, But House Balks at Outright Ban," *The Philadelphia Inquirer*, June 21, 1972, p. 1; and *Legislative Journal-House*, June 22, 1972: 3241.

59. Hobbs, one of the sponsors of the 1967 abortion reform bill, represented a heavily Catholic constituency in Pottsville. He voted in favor of HB 800 for fear of political retribution by the Catholic Conference (interview with Frederick Hobbs, Pottsville, Pa., December 14, 1992).

60. Ecenberger 1972a. See also Halva-Neubauer 1992, p. 267.

61. Ecenberger 1972b.

62. Lynch 1972.

6 Party, Discourse, and Policy

The pre-*Roe* story was one of winners and losers. To be sure, groups on both sides of the debate in New York and Pennsylvania encountered party systems that were more or less suited to their needs. But it is no coincidence that the winners in this study, pro-abortion activists in New York and antiabortion forces in Pennsylvania, framed their demands in ways that were in accord with the political conditions they faced, and that played to their respective strengths. The losers conducted campaigns that played into the hands of their opponents, either through poor use of their resources, as in New York, or by employing a discourse and a framing strategy unsuited to the political order, as in Pennsylvania. Indeed, there was nothing inevitable about the outcomes. How exactly did the winners triumph, and how did the losers contribute unintentionally to their dramatic defeats?

Winning Ways

Parties and Interests

The first thing to note is that the campaigns to change the abortion laws in both states occurred in the wake of reform movements. The two states' party systems and resulting

Table I.   1970 New York Legislature Vote on Abortion Law Repeal

	Democrats	Republicans
Senate		
For	18	13
Against	20	6
Assembly		
For	46	30
Against	24	49

political orders in the mid-1960s were radically different, however, with far more "pluralist links" available to activists in Albany than in Harrisburg.[1] Reform Democrats in New York sponsored pro-abortion laws annually from 1966 to 1970, keeping abortion policy on the legislative agenda and legitimizing the idea of reform. The bills became a rallying point that helped pro-abortion activists organize and build bipartisan support. As a result, abortion policy in New York was a function of the political parties.

As Table 1 shows, pro-abortion activists defeated the NYCC by securing the votes of legislators from both parties. Equally significant was the intra-party competition within the Democratic party, because it provided the legislative opportunity pro-abortion activists needed to get their bills introduced. It also made them attractive to the reform Democrats, who were seeking new constituencies in their ongoing struggle to gain control of the party from the regulars.[2]

Without the bi-partisan support of the Reform Democrats and Republicans pro-abortion activists in New York would not have succeeded because the issue was too controversial and the opposition of the NYCC too strong.

In Pennsylvania, abortion policy was dictated by the PCC, because by the early 1960s an unreformed party system dominated by machine politics had reasserted itself. Kitschelt (1986) refers to a "cartel of entrenched interests" having control of interest articulation in a closed system; this accurately describes the power of the PCC to defeat abortion reform resoundingly and to pass a highly restrictive abortion law despite a national trend in favor of liberalization. As Table 2 shows, the PCC, like the winning forces in New York, attracted both Democrats and Republicans. The PCC's margin of victory was far greater, however, which indicated not only that its campaign was superior to the one its opponents waged, but more significantly, showed its ability to transcend the parties, and to pass a policy that served its interests as opposed to the majority's wishes.

Since SB 38, Pennsylvania's first reform bill, was part of a broader effort to update the penal code rather than a separate party issue, as in New York, once it was killed in committee no organized pro-abortion interests existed to press for its reintroduction. Two years elapsed before another reform bill was filed, which facilitated the PCC's efforts to keep reform off the legislative agenda and to generate public support for a restrictive abortion policy. In short, although party structures alone did not decide the outcomes in New

Table 2. 1972 Pennsylvania Legislature Vote on Restrictive Abortion Policy

	Democrats	Republicans
Senate		
For	20	19
Against	3	4
House		
For	89	68
Against	15	19

York and Pennsylvania, the political orders that abortion activists in each state encountered affected the degree of access they had to the legislative process and the amount of party support available to them, both of which had a significant effect on the final vote.

Discourse

In the pre-*Roe* period, the political struggle was initially a war of words. Although antiabortion forces had the upper hand to begin with, in that they were supporting the established position, polls taken beginning in 1962 showed high majority support for therapeutic abortions. The legal discourse created by the *Griswold* decision in 1965 grounded reproductive issues in a rights-talk paradigm, which gave pro-abortion activists the language they needed to challenge the laws. By framing access to abortion within the rubric of privacy and equality, abortion supporters in a dozen states translated public support for reform into the passage of laws based on the American Law Institute's model code, which protected physicians' freedom to make medical decisions concerning therapeutic abortions and enabled a minority of women to obtain them.

In New York, the *Griswold* decision helped abortion activists persuade the reform Democrats to introduce a reform bill in 1966. The subsequent ALI-based bills gradually shifted the debate from the religious and moral/medical frameworks created in the nineteenth century to a legal/medical one, where beliefs and practices were challenged by constitutional arguments and medical facts. The bills united various groups around a rights-based story line that spoke to physicians, lawyers, and activists. In the late 1960s, radical feminists used the reproductive-rights paradigm in *Griswold* to frame the demand for repeal. The

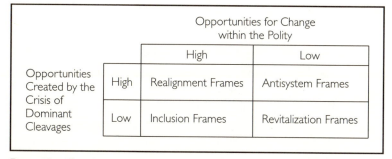

Figure 1.   Framing strategies and opportunities. *Source:* Mario Diani, "Linking Mobilization Frames and Political Opportunities," *American Sociological Review,* Vol. 61 (1996): 1059.

feminist discourse was a prime catalyst for the cognitive liberation of pro-abortion activists; it resonated with their sense that the present abortion laws were unjust, that they violated women's rights, and that the solution was to repeal them. By 1969, legislators and constituents alike agreed that only by replacing the ambiguity of reform with the simplicity of repeal would they be able to make progress. By this time the public was acquainted with the religious, medical, and legal arguments concerning abortion policy, and had been shown to be receptive to repeal. This would have been unthinkable three years earlier.

The evolution of the pre-*Roe* discourse can be understood by applying the framing strategies identified by Diani in Figure 1. In the first stage of the campaign (1965–67), pro-abortion activists in Manhattan built an alliance with the reform faction of the New York Democratic Party by placing their demands within an inclusion frame, which articulated the call for moderate reform within the medical and legal frameworks that were supported by elites both inside and outside the party.[3]

Inclusion Frames: Appropriate when dominant political alignments are strong but opportunities for independent
action are high, as was the case in New York in the first
stage of the campaign.

Realignment Frames: Appropriate when dominant political
alignments are threatened and the opportunity for independent action is high, as was the case in New York in
the second stage of the pre-*Roe* campaign.

Revitalization Frames: Appropriate when dominant political
alignments are strong, their ability to structure political
action is uncontested, and few opportunities are available
for outside political action, as was the case for pro-
abortion activists in Pennsylvania throughout the pre-*Roe*
period.

Antisystem Frames: Appropriate when dominant political
alignments are threatened but the opportunity for action
is low. This strategy did not correspond with the conditions in either New York or Pennsylvania in the pre-*Roe*
period.

In late 1968, when the political conditions in Albany
changed to their advantage, pro-abortion activists abandoned the reform position and the inclusion frame, and
adopted a realignment frame that called for the repeal of the
abortion law.[4] With the support of a bipartisan repeal coalition, activists effected this shift without de-legitimizing
established members. The demand for repeal turned the
tables on the NYCC's extreme position and challenged its
waning ability to structure the political conflict surrounding
abortion policy.

The realignment strategy was risky, but by early 1969
pro-abortion forces had little to lose. Had they failed, the
restrictive abortion law would have remained in effect.

Given the changes in the legislature and the NYCC's diminishing power to control Catholic legislators, it was a reasonable gamble. The passage of the 1970 repeal bill illustrates how a change in discourse and framing strategy can produce a very different kind of policy within a year. In a relatively short time, the basis of abortion policy had evolved from measures designed to restrict abortion to measures widening access to it.

The power of discourse to shape abortion policy was not limited to efforts to liberalize the laws. After *Griswold*, antiabortion forces drew on the Pastoral Constitution of Vatican II to revive the Church's definition of abortion as murder. By articulating abortion as a moral and religious issue, the Catholic Conference responded to the competing medical and legal definitions with a political one that mobilized antiabortion people across the country to act.[5]

In Harrisburg, after the first reform bill was introduced, the PCC employed the discourse articulated by Vatican II and the National Conference of Catholic Bishops, and began a comprehensive campaign that created an antiabortion-discourse coalition of priests, legislators, and activists.[6] Although the PCC had only to defend restrictive abortion laws already on the books, its early and vigorous organization structured the terms of the debate in Pennsylvania before its opponents had mobilized. This decreased pro-abortion activists' ability to attract the party support they needed to pursue a revitalization strategy—their most realistic alternative.[7]

Resources

Thus, the permeability of the party system and the selection of the appropriate framing and campaign strategies critically affected the outcomes of the abortion laws passed by each state. But another significant factor was the resources available to defenders and challengers in the two states. Although these resources differed, the winning forces in New York and Pennsylvania used them in similar ways in creating discourse coalitions to broaden their support, in building grassroots campaigns, and in aligning themselves with skilled legislators familiar with the institutional rules and practices needed to guide bills through committees and onto the floor.

The campaign in New York made good use of the meager resources of the pro-abortion activists, namely the literary and legal expertise of many of the early reformers. Feminists such as Lucinda Cisler, Ellen Willis, and Robin Morgan were writers and activists, and were at the center of the literary and political action of the radical women's-liberation movement. Many of the suits of the 1960s and '70s, including *Roe*, were brought by feminist attorneys who donated their legal services to pro-abortion groups. The ideological commitment of pro-abortion activists enabled them to form the grassroots communication networks that proved essential in mobilizing women. Although the concept of hierarchies and leaders was anathema to most feminist groups, many of them were founded and run by women who willy-nilly became leaders, in the sense of providing direction and developing ideas that recruited new members to various grassroots groups.

As important as these outside resources were, pro-abortion activists in New York also drew on the inside resources of groups such as the New York chapter of the ACLU, the Association for the Study of Abortion, local chapters of the League of Women Voters, and various medical and religious elites, although the support of elite groups was by no means abundant.[8] This combination of resources reflected the profiles of both the moderate and the radical activists who were part of the abortion-discourse coalition in New York. It included physicians and public-health advocates who were in favor of limited reform as well as radicals dedicated to the repeal of all abortion laws.

Pro-abortion activists in New York benefited immeasurably from the leadership of Assemblywoman Constance Cook, who coordinated the coalition of liberal Democrat and Republican legislators, abortion activists, feminists, and the various church and civic groups in both regions of the state. Cook was also sufficiently experienced to accept the give-and-take nature of legislative bargaining. Though the compromises she accepted prompted some feminists to abandon the bill, they brought some conservative Republicans into the fold. When the political window opened in the spring of 1970, pro-repeal forces slipped through.

In Pennsylvania, organization, resources, and timing contributed equally to the success of the PCC. In addition to maintaining its diocesan campaign, the PCC broadened its support with the creation of Pennsylvanians for Human Life and reached out to nonsectarian groups, such as Women Concerned for the Unborn Child. Unlike its counterpart in New York, the PCC took abortion-reform efforts seriously from the start. Though it had fewer problems in terms of consistent leadership and other major legislative issues to contend with, what distinguished the PCC from the NYCC were its long-term strategy and its superb use of the dioceses to link networks of antiabortion grassroots groups across the state.

The considerable resources of the PCC gave antiabortion grassroots activists legislative access, legal counsel, office staff, meeting places, and, most important, a direct link to large numbers of parishioners every Sunday, which helped them to recruit new members. Antiabortion activists also mobilized support through the Catholic press, which provided an alternative to the mainstream news media, which they felt were biased against them.[9] The PCC was aligned with Martin Mullen, chairman of the Pennsylvania House Appropriations Committee; Mullen, like Cook, used his influence and knowledge of legislative procedures to line up the votes. Mullen's fiery oratory and passionate advocacy of restrictive abortion policy aided antiabortion forces in Pennsylvania by highlighting the moral aspects of the issue, a strategy that complemented the discourse articulated by the PCC from the start. Mullen was to the Pennsylvania forces what Cook was to those in New York: a legislative champion. Although Governor Shapp eventually vetoed HB 800, antiabortion forces had nonetheless succeeded in establishing the parameters of the pre-*Roe* debate—and, as it turned out, the post-*Roe* debate as well.[10]

Losing Approaches

Parties and Interests

Why antiabortion forces in New York and pro-abortion activists in Pennsylvania lost in the pre-*Roe* period can also be understood by examining the factors discussed above: the political climates within which they operated, the discourses and framing strategies they employed, and the way they used their resources. Had the losers maximized their advantages, they probably would have achieved results that, while not ideal from their point of view, would have been less damaging to their cause than what resulted.

In New York, the NYCC used its political clout to kill reform bills in committee, but eventually pro-abortion reformers succeeded in getting the reform bill onto the floor in 1968. This was the first indication that the NYCC was losing its control of the issue. This, coupled with the legislative changes in Albany after the November elections in that year, should have prompted the NYCC to expand its campaign against reform by building bipartisan support for restrictive abortion policy, as opposed to simply killing bills in committee or defeating them on the floor. The NYCC's miscalculation was especially damaging because, unlike the PCC, it had to cope with political opposition to its abortion policy, a consequence of the open party system in New York. Beginning in 1967, the NYCC's abortion policy was challenged by various churches and liberal organizations, especially the Clergy Consultation Service, whose public campaign in favor of abortion reform broadened the debate and countered the NYCC's claim of exclusive religious authority. When Cardinal Spellman issued a pastoral letter urging legislators to defeat the reform bill in 1967, a joint statement issued by the New York City Protestant Council and the Association of Reform Rabbis denounced the Church's position on abortion.[11]

Although pro-abortion activists in Pennsylvania also faced an uphill political battle, had they aligned with legislators who opposed the PCC's reproductive policies, they might have attracted support for a reform bill, especially given the bipartisan sponsorship of SB 38. Such bills would have provided their campaign with legitimacy, given them access to the policy process, and helped them build a bipartisan coalition of groups to generate support for reform, which proved critical to the activists' success in New York. Instead, pro-abortion activists in Pennsylvania opted to concentrate on a direct service approach, which consumed their meager resources and sidetracked them from securing legislative support. Further, their disagreements about the most effective way to deal with the problem of securing safe abortions hampered their political effectiveness and reinforced the PCC's unwavering opposition to abortion reform. As a result of all these factors, pro-abortion forces in Pennsylvania remained fragmented until 1972, when the first public hearings on abortion were held. By then, the PCC had been organizing against abortion reform for five years.

Strategies, Discourse, and Resources

The losing forces in New York and Pennsylvania faced different challenges in terms of the framing strategies available to them. In Albany, the NYCC had no room for compromise: It was required to defend the established position on abortion policy and was unable to modify its framing strategy, as its opponents did, when the political order changed. Yet it had the resources necessary to mount a broad-based campaign to defeat both reform and repeal bills had it been better organized.

The NYCC recognized the importance of attracting non-Catholics to the cause, especially given the bitter multidenominational battle over the Blaine amendment. Despite this, it did not made a sustained effort to do so, as the PCC had done in Pennsylvania. This was especially damaging in the upstate region, where there were fewer Catholics, and where legislators were more inclined to respond to their constituents, as pro-abortion groups in the region had demonstrated. As Senator Manfred Ohrenstein remarked, "the eventual vote on the bill was a remarkable triumph of grassroots pressure."[12]

Its efforts to mobilize the Catholic community were limited as well. Although it worked with the Knights of

Columbus to mobilize against any changes in the abortion law, the NYCC failed to implement a diocesan plan to coordinate local grassroots efforts with its legislative campaign in Albany. It appointed "abortion coordinators" in each of its eight dioceses, but the positions were not always filled, and their high turnover rate impaired the program's ability to organize on the local level.[13] Further, it failed to use the New York Right to Life Committee to mobilize rural constituents, the way the PCC did with the PHL. As Golden observed, "They didn't nudge us, we nudged them."[14]

In essence, the NYCC miscalculated the significance of Governor Rockefeller's re-election and the subsequent political changes that followed, and concluded that its ability to defeat reform bills, let alone repeal, was not in serious jeopardy. By the time it realized its error, after the Senate had voted in favor of repeal, it was too late to line up the forces in the Assembly to defeat the bill. The changing political climate, the absence of a grassroots campaign, and its underestimation of the support pro-abortion forces had built over its five-year campaign proved to be the NYCC's undoing.

The chief resources of pro-abortion supporters in Pennsylvania, as in the rest of the country, were the various medical, political, legal, and feminist discourses that had evolved in the 1960s. Given the closed party system, however, and the alliance between the Democratic Party and the PCC on reproductive issues, abortion supporters' best bet would have been a revitalization strategy.[15] Such an approach, based on challengers' attempts to align themselves with existing forces, would have helped them to organize and coordinate activists. It also would have facilitated the creation of a reform-discourse coalition, which proved essential to the success of pro-abortion forces in New York.

Instead, a year into their campaign, abortion supporters embraced a feminist discourse with the introduction of a repeal bill, which in effect initiated an antisystem strategy. This approach is suitable where established interests are vulnerable, but this was clearly not the case in Pennsylvania: The PCC dominated the abortion debate from start to finish. Had pro-abortion forces in Pennsylvania been as well organized as their allies in New York, this framing strategy, while risky, might have strengthened their position.[16] But lacking a longstanding pro-abortion campaign in the state, which would have familiarized the public with the idea of reform, the call for repeal backfired. It played into the hands of the PCC, which used the bill's radical call for repeal to justify HB 800's equally radical call for the prohibition of all abortions.

The differences in the political structures in New York and Pennsylvania made it unlikely that pro-abortion activists in Pennsylvania could have succeeded in passing an abortion-repeal bill similar to New York's. Had they obtained early party backing, however, or been sufficiently organized to have built interest-group support for reform in the initial stages of the campaign, they would have had a reasonable chance of preventing the passage of HB 800, and possibly of passing the kind of reform legislation enacted by other states in this period. Had they defeated the PCC in 1972, it's unlikely that antiabortion forces would have continued to shape abortion policy in Pennsylvania and the rest of the country after 1973, especially in light of Governor Shapp's support for wide access to abortion. It's true that pro-abortion forces in Pennsylvania faced an uphill battle with few resources, but it's also true that they squandered the one resource they possessed that might have prevented their defeat: the pre-*Roe* discourses.

When the New York and Pennsylvania cases are compared in light of the factors of systemic permeability, discourse, resources, and strategies, we can see why they passed radically different abortion policies. In each case, both challengers and defenders had the potential to substantially shape the outcome. The winners maximized their advantages; the losers failed to do so.

Of the four players in this battle, the PCC had the most in its favor to begin with, and its opponents had the least. At first glance, the policy outcome in Pennsylvania reflects this. But though the pro-abortion activists had little influence with the party system they encountered, they had the power to hinder the PCC and limit the latter's success. In New York, the same imbalance of power between the Catholic Conference and pro-abortion activists existed at the outset, but within five years the activists had managed to reverse it by aligning themselves with the reform Democrats and building a reform-discourse coalition that laid the foundation for a shift to repeal. Due to a combination of political developments, disorganization, and a poor use of its resources, the NYCC, one of the most powerful Catholic Conferences in the country, squandered its opportunities and suffered a dramatic defeat.

Notes

1. Kitschelt 1986, p. 63.

2. In their analysis of the pre-*Roe* period, Mooney and Lee (1995) found that district-level party competition was negatively associated with the likelihood of a state reforming its laws. Due to the aggregate nature of their study, however, they did not address the issue of *intra-party* competition, which was a key factor in the New York case.

3. Central to inclusion strategies are rhetorical devices used to articulate new political actors' intentions to be recognized as legitimate members of the polity. The more these devices emphasize the similarities between old and new members, and downplay the differences between them, the higher the chance of challenging forces' acceptance (Diani 1996, p. 57).

4. Diani defines realignment strategies as those where challengers take positions that create new alignments without effecting a "global delegitimization of the established members and procedures of the polity" (ibid., p. 1056).

5. See Luker 1984, Ch. 6, and Ginsberg 1989, Ch. 4, for the emergence of pre-*Roe* antiabortion campaigns in California and North Dakota, respectively. See also Faux 1988, Ch. 11 for pre-*Roe* antiabortion actions in Texas.

6. Minutes from PCC right-to-life coordinators' meeting, April 2, 1971, and PCC and diocesan right-to-life coordinators meeting, June 11, 1971. Files of the PCC.

7. This strategy calls for challengers to work with established organizations to try to redirect their goals. Given the strength of the PCC, this strategy represented pro-abortion activists' best chance of effecting change, or at least of preventing the PCC from completely dominating abortion policy.

8. Staggenborg 1991, p. 27.

9. The view that the press was slanted to the liberal side and in favor of abortion was expressed to me by scores of antiabortion activists I interviewed in New York, Pennsylvania, and Washington, D.C.

10. The post-*Roe* period is discussed in the next chapter.

11. Lader 1973, p. 59.

12. Lader 1973, p. 124.

13. The above description is based on Traina 1975, p. 16b.

14. Shapiro 1972, p. 10.

15. Although this approach, where challengers align with established members of the polity "in order to redirect their goals and revitalize their structures from within," may not have succeeded in passing a reform bill, according to Diani's typology it would have been "the least unsuccessful" and probably would have prevented the passage of HB 800 (1996, p. 1057).

16. As demonstrated in New York, a feminist discourse can move the debate to the next stage, but it is unsuitable for generating broad-based support because of the challenge it poses to traditional alliances, as well as to social customs. On this point, see Gelb and Palley's discussion of role equity versus role change (1987, Ch. 1). The case of the equal-rights amendment in Pennsylvania illustrates the efficacy of moderation. In 1971, Pennsylvania became one of the first states to ratify the ERA. There was no significant opposition to it, largely because of the low-key strategy of its supporters, who made a concerted effort to downplay the importance of the bill. Interview with Gerald Kaufman, June 17, 1993. See also Linda J. Wharton 1991, pp. 159–60.

7 After *Roe:* The Pendulum Swings Back

After *Roe,* abortion politics in America were transformed. The decision put abortion policy on the national agenda and expanded the influence of the women's movement; later it did the same for the pro-life movement.[1] *Roe* decriminalized early abortions: without it, most states would have retained their restrictive abortion laws and many women who wanted abortions would have had difficulty obtaining legal ones. In terms of the development of abortion policy in America, however, the chief significance of the *Roe* decision was the national debate it inaugurated, for the legal and feminist discourses based on women's rights that were institutionalized by *Roe* came into collision with the moral discourse based on the sanctity of life advanced by pro-life forces.[2]

After 1973 the term "pro-abortion" was replaced by "pro-choice," a rhetorical shift that reflected a feminist sensibility based on new roles for women outside the home and family, and complemented the emerging campaign to ratify the equal-rights amendment. The term enabled them to portray themselves as the defenders of choice, which was more in line with their position in support of women's rights.[3] It also distanced them from the unsavory image of being in favor of abortion for its own sake, which was especially useful once their opponents began a campaign featuring pictures of fetuses. Meanwhile, the term "right-to-life," which was favored by opposing grassroots groups, was gradually replaced on the national level by the simpler name "pro-life," which also asked the public to choose between the rights of a woman who did not want the fetus she was carrying and the right of the fetus to live.[4]

Despite *Roe's* central holding—that a woman's right to choose an abortion was a fundamental one protected by the Constitution—regulations governing access to it remained a state issue, as they had been before 1973. As a result, legislatures and courts on the state and national level became embroiled in an ongoing battle between pro-choice and pro-life forces over the meaning of *Roe*. And after 1973 the strategies of the two sides were reversed, with pro-choice forces defending the status quo—the changes brought by *Roe*—and pro-life groups challenging it. In the early 1970s pro-choice supporters continued to win in the courts, while pro-life supporters succeeded in passing restrictive laws on the state level that gradually limited women's access to abortion. As early as 1976, however, pro-life forces expanded their influence to the judicial arena, and their opponents' control of abortion policy began to erode.

This trend continued into the 1980s, when pro-life groups benefited from the Reagan administration's bureaucratic initiatives, such as those governing Title X funds, and by the appointments of conservative judges to the federal judiciary.[5] Pro-choice forces were increasingly on the defensive. In 1989 pro-life forces were vindicated by the Supreme Court's decision in *Webster v. Reproductive Health Services,* which increased the power of the states to regulate abortion.[6] The trajectory of the issue during this period (1973–89) was especially evident in Pennsylvania, where the state legislature enacted four abortion-control acts that pitted the legislature against the courts.

Roe v. Wade

The breadth of the decision in *Roe v. Wade* was shocking to both sides. In the words of Lawrence Lader, a pro-abortion activist, "It came like a thunderbolt on January 22, 1973—a decision from the United States Supreme Court that went beyond what anyone had predicted."[7] A pro-life activist in California was similarly stunned: "Well, I think just about like everyone else in the [Support Life] league, we felt as though the bottom had been pulled out from under us. It was an incredible thing. I couldn't believe it. In fact, I didn't. For a couple of months I kept thinking, 'It can't be right, I'm not hearing what I'm hearing.'"[8]

Despite the incredulity even of activists, the *Roe* decision was in some ways a logical extension of *Griswold,* and of the Supreme Court's 1972 decision in *Eisenstadt v. Baird,* which held that a Massachusetts law prohibiting the distribution of contraceptive devices to unmarried people was unconstitutional because it violated the right to privacy.[9] *Griswold* had applied the right to privacy to enable a married couple to buy contraceptives without state interference; *Eisenstadt* expanded this definition of privacy to single people. *Roe* extended the definition of privacy a step further, to include abortion. Furthermore, the decision essentially enabled women to obtain legal abortions up to the 24th week of pregnancy with few state restrictions, precisely what the 1970 N.Y. abortion repeal law had done 3 years earlier.

While the Court held in *Roe* that a woman's right to privacy included the right to choose to terminate a pregnancy, it also maintained that the states had a direct interest at a later point: "The pregnant woman cannot be isolated in her privacy. She carries an embryo, and later a fetus. . . . The situation is therefore inherently different from marital privacy

. . . or procreation. . . . As we have intimated above, it is reasonable and appropriate for a State to decide that at some point in time another interest, that of the health of the mother or that of potential human life, becomes significantly involved. The woman's privacy is no longer sole and any right of privacy she possesses must be measured accordingly."[10]

In *Roe,* the Court employed the trimester construct used by physicians to balance the rights of women, doctors, and the states, and to determine whose rights would prevail during the nine months of pregnancy. In the first trimester the woman's right to privacy and her physician's right to practice medicine without government intrusion outweighed those of the states: The woman was free to choose to terminate her pregnancy, and her physician was free to perform the abortion. In the second trimester of pregnancy the rights of the woman and her physician still prevailed, but the Court recognized the right of the states to regulate abortions for the purposes of protecting maternal health. Complications are more likely in second-trimester abortions, and if the state could demonstrate that the woman's health might be impaired, it could require that the abortion be performed in a fully equipped hospital, as opposed to a clinic. In the third trimester, the state's interest in promoting potential human life was paramount: The state could proscribe abortions, except when the woman's life or health was endangered.

The trimester approach accommodated the common-law distinction between legal and illegal abortions that allowed women to have abortions until quickening—approximately the fifth month of pregnancy—with little penalty. At the same time, it let the Court accommodate the belief that once the fetus was viable, the state had the obligation to protect it. With its reference to "potential life," the Court recognized the interests of the states in regulating maternal health, and by extension fetal health. "The State does have an important and legitimate interest in preserving and protecting the health of the pregnant woman [and] it has still *another* important and legitimate interest in protecting the potentiality of human life," the Court ruled.[11] The Supreme Court's recognition of the states' interest in protecting potential life would soon become a central argument advanced by pro-life forces in advocating restrictions on second-trimester abortions.[12] Their more immediate aim, however, was to pass restrictions on women's access to first-trimester abortions. In *Doe v. Bolton,* the companion case to *Roe,* the Court specifically addressed the ways in which Georgia had attempted to limit women's access to abortions.

The *Doe* decision was important to the development of post-*Roe* abortion policy because it specifically addressed the kinds of state regulations that had been the subject of debate before 1973.[13] The issue in *Doe* was how the state of Georgia regulated access to abortions, and what kinds of restrictions states could apply, as opposed to the broader issues of fundamental rights that were addressed in *Roe.* Georgia was one of the first states in the pre-*Roe* period to pass an ALI-based abortion law. Unlike the Texas statute, the Georgia law, passed in 1968, allowed abortions when the woman's physical and mental health was endangered. However, it also established a series of procedural requirements that had to be met before an abortion could be performed, and these requirements were what the Court addressed.[14]

The first requirement—that abortions must be performed in hospitals approved by the Joint Commission on Accreditation of Hospitals in Georgia—was struck down because other medical procedures were legally performed in licensed hospitals without this accreditation. In addition, the Court

questioned the necessity of having early abortions performed in hospitals, and concluded that the state's interest
in protecting maternal health did not require this. Next, the
Court took issue with the requirement that a hospital committee approve all abortions; the Court decided that the
approval of a woman's physician was enough to insure her
right to receive medical care without further scrutiny. The
Court also concluded that a physician's decision to perform
a therapeutic abortion was sufficient to protect the state's
interest in protecting fetal life.

The third challenged requirement was that two doctors
concur with the woman's physician, and here, too, the
Court deferred to the attending physician's judgment.[15]
Finally, the Court considered Georgia's residency requirement, which had been included because some legislators
feared that without it the state would become an "abortion
mecca."[16] The Court struck down this requirement as well,
based on the privileges and immunities clause in Article IV
of the Constitution.[17]

The fact that *Doe* addressed the substance of Georgia's
restrictions rather than simply invalidating them was an
important point. The Court's decision was interpreted to
mean that *Roe* did not proscribe first-trimester restrictions if
they could be shown to further the state's interests.[18] This
encouraged states to enact a variety of abortion restrictions
that fell into four broad categories: reporting and licensing
requirements; consent provisions; fetal-viability guidelines;
and the use of public facilities and funds for abortion.[19] All
of these found their way into the 1974 Abortion Control Act
enacted in Pennsylvania, which continued its pre-*Roe* tradition of passing restrictive abortion legislation.

The Abortion Control Act of 1974

Pennsylvania was not alone in passing restrictive abortion laws just one year after *Roe*. Massachusetts and Missouri did the same.[20] The 1974 Pennsylvania Abortion Control Act, SB 1318, shared many of the provisions of the Missouri act. These included viability regulations that physicians were required to follow and rules governing informed consent (a woman requesting an abortion had to be told the details of the procedure), spousal consent, unless the woman's life was endangered, and parental permission for an abortion if the woman was a minor. But Pennsylvania significantly expanded restrictions on abortion by prohibiting the public funding of abortions unless the woman's health or life was in danger—a restriction that proved to be widely popular on the state level in the period after *Roe*.[21]

The punitive nature of the funding and consent provisions reflected the attempts of pro-life forces in Pennsylvania to retain the moral imperative they'd had in the pre-*Roe* period. As noted in Chapter Five, one of the discourse strategies the PCC pursued in the 1960s was to cast doubt on the legitimacy of claims of rape, incest, and mental health as grounds for therapeutic abortions by portraying women and physicians who made these claims as untrustworthy. The consent provisions of SB 1318 cast a similar shadow on women, and implicitly questioned their ability to make an informed decision on abortion without a state-mandated explanation of the procedure.

Despite *Roe*, both houses passed SB 1318 by large margins.[22] Unlike HB 800, which initially banned all abortions, SB 1318 was considered a more reasonable approach by many legislators, in that the bill attempted to enact restrictions rather than an outright ban. In addition, some legislators felt more comfortable creating abortion policy within federal guidelines that would be checked by the courts.[23] By voting in favor of restrictions, many concluded, they would end up with an abortion bill that would satisfy most of their constituents. Although the early introduction of SB 1318 compelled legislators to vote before the November election, they were less concerned with crossing Governor Shapp in his second and last term.[24]

The passage of SB 1318 and the easy override of Shapp's veto reflected the continuing strength of pro-life forces in Pennsylvania.[25] The years of organization before *Roe* had enabled antiabortion activists to translate the resentment of people who felt that the decision had gone too far into support for restrictive abortion laws. As one of the first major post-*Roe* abortion bills to be passed in the country, the Pennsylvania legislation laid the groundwork for attempts in other states to limit access to abortion. As expected, the act was immediately challenged in court, but the precedent of the legislature restricting access to early as well as late abortions had been established.

Within the next five years, the courts ruled on the constitutionality of several of the act's provisions. In the first case, *Planned Parenthood Association v. Fitzpatrick* (1975), a district court deemed several provisions of the 1974 Abortion Control Act to be unconstitutional.[26] The court held that spousal- and parental-consent provisions violated women's rights to privacy, and that the prohibition of public funding for nontherapeutic abortions violated the equal-protection clause. It also struck down Pennsylvania's definition of viability, which necessitated a standard of care, on the grounds of vagueness.[27] Several provisions, however, were upheld including those regarding licensing, reporting, and medical procedures.[28]

In its 1976 decision in *Planned Parenthood of Central Missouri v. Danforth,* the Supreme Court handed down its first major abortion decision since *Roe*.[29] In *Danforth,* laws requiring women to obtain spousal or parental consent before obtaining an abortion were held to be violations of their rights, but informed consent was upheld. The most significant aspect of the *Danforth* decision, in terms of future attempts to restrict abortion, concerned the Court's acceptance of Missouri's definition of viability as "when the life of the unborn child may be continued indefinitely outside the womb by natural or artificial life-supportive systems."[30] Without imposing a standard of care, as the 1974 Pennsylvania act had, Missouri succeeded in gaining constitutional grounding for a definition of viability not bound by a trimester framework.

This was significant, because it signaled the Supreme Court's later willingness to allow states to enact other restrictions on first-trimester abortions, such as prohibiting public funding of nontherapeutic abortions (*Beal v. Doe* and *Maher v. Roe*) and allowing states to limit the kinds of abortions poor women could obtain in public hospitals (*Poelker v. Doe*).[31] These decisions were without regard to the trimester framework, which had been previously understood to prohibit first-trimester restrictions, with the exception of licensing requirements for medical workers and facilities. *Danforth* also helped pave the way for the Court's application of the "undue burden" standard discussed below, which played a crucial role in the Court's major abortion decisions in the 1980s.

Despite *Danforth,* the Supreme Court continued throughout the 1970s to protect physicians' ability to practice medicine without undue state interference by striking down ambiguous legislative definitions of the medical conditions and guidelines governing standards of care. In *Colautti v. Franklin,* the Court struck down Pennsylvania's definition of viability and its attendant standard-of-care requirements, as described in the 1974 Abortion Control Act, on the grounds of vagueness, because the section used the terms "viable" and "may be viable" to describe the physician's duty to the state.[32] The Court found that such ambiguity could imperil the practitioner and enable the state to prosecute the physician, which went against its intention to allow the physician to make medical judgments with no institutional interference in the first trimester: "*Roe* stressed repeatedly the central role of the physician, both in consulting with the woman whether or not to have an abortion, and in determining how any abortion was to be carried out. We indicated that up to the points where important state interests provide compelling justifications for intervention, 'the abortion decision in all its aspects is inherently, and primarily, a medical decision.'"[33]

Despite these gains, by the late 1970s pro-life forces across the country were at a crossroads. While some parts of the movement concentrated on passing restrictive laws, many activists were more committed to passing a human-life amendment to the Constitution, an effort sponsored by the National Conference of Catholic Bishops in 1975 as part of its Pastoral Plan for Pro-Life Activity.[34] The proposed amendment described the "right to life" as a fundamental right protected by the Fifth and Fourteenth Amendments— one that was superseded only by a pregnant woman's right to have an abortion if her life was in danger. Given the difficulty of amending the Constitution, it eventually became apparent to pro-life leaders that this was a poor use of their resources.

Another misstep was pro-life's brief alliance with evangelical and other conservative forces which it formed in the late 1970s, because the latter offered direct-mail and tele-marketing techniques in exchange for the electoral support of pro-life organizations and their valuable lists of committed members. Supporters' lack of enthusiasm for a broader social agenda favored by conservatives persuaded pro-life leaders to concentrate exclusively on abortion, which was by far the most politically salient issue of the pro-family platform. The successful passage of the Hyde Amendments in the late 1970s, which restricted the spending of Medicaid funds for nontherapeutic abortions, as well as the decisions in *Maher* and *Poelker, Beal,* suggested that the future lay in drafting legislation to establish the parameters of states' rights to regulate abortions, as opposed to simply pitting a woman's right to have an abortion against the right of the fetus to be born.

For pro-life forces, restrictions on abortions in the first trimester, which is when most abortions are performed, were desirable not because they significantly reduced the number of abortions[35] but because early restrictions increased state control over nontherapeutic abortions—precisely the kind pro-life advocates most abhorred. In addition, they articulated the moral misgivings about elective abortions that many people continued to have after *Roe,* a sentiment pro-life forces exploited to generate support for more laws.[36]

More Restrictions

In an effort to expand state control over abortion policy, state legislators, starting in the late 1970s, began introducing increasingly restrictive and comprehensive bills that contained both old and new restrictions and went beyond what the courts had deemed to be constitutional.[37] In 1983 the Supreme Court applied the *Roe* doctrine to three cases involving restrictions on first- and second-trimester abortions that had been enacted by the states. In the first of these, *City of Akron v. Akron Center for Reproductive Health*, the Court struck down five sections of the city's abortion ordinance: informed- and parental-consent provisions, which the Court deemed intrusive; a hospital requirement for second-trimester abortions; a requirement of a twenty-four-hour waiting period; and regulations concerning the disposal of fetal remains.[38]

Equally significant was Justice Sandra Day O'Connor's dissent, which provided a new framework for pro-life forces to use in drafting restrictive legislation. Although the Court struck down most sections of Akron's abortion law, O'Connor's use of an "undue burden" standard became the benchmark for future restrictions:[39] "Our recent cases indicate that a regulation imposed on 'a lawful abortion' is not unconstitutional unless it unduly burdens the right to seek an abortion. . . . In my view, this 'unduly burdensome' standard should be applied to the challenged regulations throughout the entire pregnancy without reference to the particular 'stage' of pregnancy involved. If the particular regulation does not 'unduly burde[n]' the fundamental right . . . then our evaluation of that regulation is limited to our determination that the regulation rationally relates to a legitimate state purpose."[40]

Another hopeful sign for pro-life forces was that when it came to procedural restrictions, the Court showed a willingness to allow the states greater leeway in protecting their interests. In *Planned Parenthood Association of Kansas City, Missouri v. Ashcroft*, the companion case to *Akron*, the Court once again struck down the second-trimester hospital requirement, but upheld three sections of Missouri's 1981 act, including one that required the presence of a second doctor during any abortion performed after viability.[41]

In the third abortion case decided in 1983, *Simopolous v. Virginia,* the Court upheld Virginia's hospital requirement for second-trimester abortions. In this case, unlike in *Akron* and *Ashcroft,* the law's definition of "hospital" included outpatient surgical hospitals. In practice, since none of these hospitals did second-trimester abortions, the only place a woman in Virginia could get an abortion after the twelfth week of pregnancy was in a full-fledged hospital, which made the procedure more expensive.[42] But, as the Court's majority indicated in *Maher* and *Poelker,* the Court did not consider cost a factor in its decisions concerning the constitutionality of public funding restrictions for elective abortions.

Although pro-choice forces retained more support for unrestricted access to abortion than they lost, these decisions by no means represented a clear-cut victory for them, because they showed that the Supreme Court's support of a fundamental abortion right was split. To pro-life forces, the decisions suggested that restrictions that were rationally related to a state's interest and that did not impose an undue burden on the pregnant woman would be upheld for early as well as late abortions.[43] In addition, it seemed possible that restrictions that erred on the side of caution might be upheld, as long as they did not depart significantly from accepted medical practice,[44] a standard that had guided the Court since *Roe.*[45]

By the early 1980s, a national pro-life movement had emerged. Pro-life forces on the state level increasingly relied on national organizations such as the American Life League, the American Life Lobby, and Americans United for Life to draft restrictive abortion legislation that could withstand constitutional challenge. As a result, the role played by individual legislators aligned with national organizations was elevated at the expense of interest groups and parties.[46]

The strategy used in Pennsylvania in the early 1980s by Stephen Freind and Gregg Cunningham, two Republican representatives, was illustrative of this new direction.[47] The package of bills they introduced in 1981 incorporated revised provisions of Pennsylvania's 1974 Abortion Control Act, such as more detailed informed-consent and parental requirements, which had previously been struck down, and added new regulations concerning paternal notice and abortions after the point of viability.[48] The significance of the new provisions was that they applied to first- and second-trimester abortions respectively, and increased the number of state-imposed restrictions on early abortions that had been established in *Fitzpatrick* and *Danforth*.

The informed-consent and post-viability provisions were also an attempt to expand state control at the expense of physicians and women. The informed-consent provision required doctors to provide the woman with lists of agencies offering alternatives to abortion, to explain the medical risks involved, and to show her photographs of fetuses at different gestational ages.[49] The viability provision interfered with doctors' ability to practice medicine in the manner they chose; it required the physician to choose the abortion technique most likely to preserve the life of the fetus, except when the woman's life would be endangered.[50]

Although Governor Richard Thornburgh vetoed the 1981 bill because he suspected that certain provisions were unconstitutional, the following year he signed the Abortion Control Act of 1982, which accommodated his concerns while retaining the main consent and viability provisions discussed earlier.[51] Several states had drafted restrictive abortion laws after *Roe*, and the Supreme Court had upheld some of them in the early 1980s.[52] The 1982 Pennsylvania Abortion Control Act expanded some of the provisions of the laws that had been upheld, including informed- and parental-consent requirements, and the requirement of a second physician for post-viability abortions, which had been established in *Ashcroft*. It also introduced new ones including labeling requirements for abortifacients and guidelines governing the filing of lawsuits in instances of wrongful life and birth.[53]

Like the 1974 and 1981 Abortion Control Acts, the 1982 act was designed to test and push the limits of *Roe*. It was challenged, and four years later the Supreme Court ruled on it in *Thornburgh v. American College of Obstetricians & Gynecologists*.[54] Although the Court had earlier dealt with various aspects of the challenged provisions—standard of care, informed consent, a second-physician requirement for post-viability abortions, and reporting and information requirements, the 1982 act attempted to expand the parameters of these restrictions.[55] *Thornburgh* provided the Court with its first opportunity to review a comprehensive law since *Danforth*, ten years earlier.

The first few pages of the majority opinion reviewed the abortion laws passed in Pennsylvania since 1974, with the majority of the Court questioning the intent of the Pennsylvania Legislature[56] and suggesting that the provisions had been designed to intimidate women, not to help them make an informed decision: "Appellants claim that the statutory provisions before us today further legitimate compelling interests of the Commonwealth. Close analysis of those provisions, however, shows that they wholly subordinate constitutional privacy interests and concerns with maternal health in an effort to deter a woman from making a decision, that, with her physician, is hers to make."[57]

Citing the constitutional principles established in *Roe*, the Supreme Court affirmed the lower court's ruling and struck down all six challenged provisions.

In his dissent, Justice Byron White, joined by Justice William Rehnquist and in part by Warren Burger and O'Connor, accused the Court of misconstruing the states' interests in regulating abortion policy: "The majority's opinion evinces no deference toward the State's legitimate policy. Rather, the majority makes it clear from the outset that it simply disapproves of any attempt by Pennsylvania to legislate in this area. The history of the state legislature's decade-long effort to pass a constitutional abortion statute is recounted as if it were evidence of some sinister conspiracy."[58]

Given the Court's recent application of *Roe* in *Ashcroft* and *Simopolous*, its decision in *Thornburgh* indicated that a woman's right to abortion still outweighed the state's interests in protecting maternal health and potential life, but only by one vote. In some ways, *Thornburgh*'s 5-to-4 margin was as important in explaining the development of abortion policy in the late 1980s as was the substance of the decision.[59] It demonstrated a deep disagreement in the Supreme Court over the balance between a woman's right to abortion and states' rights to regulate policy, and, more important, over whether the woman's right was fundamental.

The following year, undeterred by the *Thornburgh* decision, pro-life forces in Pennsylvania drafted the 1987 Abortion Control Act. They attempted to rectify the requirements the Court had found objectionable in *Thornburgh*, decreasing the amount and kind of information physicians were required to report to the state and to women seeking abortions, and pushing back the week in which physicians were required to perform viability tests.[60] The 1987 act introduced a new regulation, a prohibition on the use of legal-services funds for abortion cases, and recycled the paternal-notification requirement from the 1981 bill, thus continuing the gradualist approach they had employed since the early 1980s.[61]

In terms of the wider conflict over abortion policy, the main importance of the restrictions implemented by numerous states, including Pennsylvania, was that they represented the increasing strength of the pro-life forces. By 1989, the number of states providing public funding for nontherapeutic abortions had dropped to thirteen, twenty states had enacted some type of parental or spousal notification, fourteen had parental-consent requirements, and thirty-seven prohibited public funding for nontherapeutic abortions.[62] In Pennsylvania most women had to travel to another county for an abortion.[63] The restrictions reflected the moral underpinnings of the pro-life discourse and put pro-choice forces on the defensive.

Webster and *Casey*

A decade of pro-life activity was vindicated by the 1989 Supreme Court decision in *Webster v. Reproductive Health Services.* In *Webster,* the Court ruled on the constitutionality of several provisions of Missouri's 1986 abortion law that were at the center of the post-*Roe* debate: the establishment of fetal-viability procedures; a definition of when life begins; and limitations on the use of public funds, employees, and facilities for abortion and abortion counseling.

Webster was for pro-life forces what *Roe* had been for pro-choice advocates: It established a constitutional framework governing a woman's right to abortion. The crucial difference was the Court's changing interpretation of that right. In *Roe*, a majority of the justices interpreted abortion to be a fundamental constitutional right; in *Webster* a new majority disagreed. For the first time since 1973, a majority on the Supreme Court had given constitutional approval to the spirit of the laws pro-lifers favored: those based on the belief that life begins at conception. In *Webster*, the Court upheld the ban on the use of public employees, hospitals, and funds for abortion counseling, and for performing abortions except when the woman's life was endangered. It also upheld the requirement that physicians perform viability tests on fetuses of twenty or more weeks of age, and let stand the preamble to the Missouri act stating that life begins at conception, and that the unborn have interests that are to be protected.

In upholding these restrictions, the Court put aside the trimester framework, which favored women's rights over state efforts to regulate abortion in the first trimester, and applied the "undue burden" standard, which expanded states' powers over abortion from the onset of pregnancy. This was significant because it represented a shift away from the dependence the Court had placed on physicians' expertise and toward an expansion of states' power to enact regulations that limited physicians' ability to decide when an abortion was appropriate.[64]

This deference to the states resonated in Pennsylvania, which was the first state after *Webster* to pass new abortion restrictions. "The scariest feeling was right after *Webster*," recalled Denise Neary, director of the Pennsylvania Pro-Life Federation. "It was like the eyes of the nation were upon us. There were all these what-ifs: What if we can't get the same majorities as we got before? Will that be considered a failure? We just felt a real responsibility—a burden I guess, is the way to phrase it. Everybody was looking at us. And we were going to fail the whole movement if we didn't come through."[65]

In October, three months after the *Webster* decision was announced, pro-life forces in Pennsylvania succeeded in passing the 1989 Abortion Control Act, the fourth major restrictive abortion bill since *Roe*. The act's main provisions were an informed consent provision that required a twenty-four–hour waiting period before an abortion could be performed, a spousal notification requirement, and a parental-consent provision that had been in the 1988 act. Once again, pro-choice forces filed suit and the case was eventually heard by the Supreme Court.

The Supreme Court's 1992 ruling in *Planned Parenthood of Southeastern Pennsylvania v. Casey* can be seen as a compromise between *Roe* and *Webster*.[66] The crucial question was the one the Court had spoken to in *Roe:* Where was the dividing line between women's liberty to control their reproductive functions and states' rights to regulate maternal health and protect potential life? In *Casey* the Court upheld *Roe*'s finding that women have the right to first-trimester abortions with limited state interference, but it also upheld the states' rights to regulate abortion from the outset of pregnancy:

> It must be stated at the outset and with clarity that *Roe*'s essential holding . . . has three parts. First is a recognition of the right of the woman to choose to have an abortion before viability and to obtain it without undue interference from the State. Before viability the State's interests are not strong enough to support a prohibition of abortion or the imposition of a substantial obstacle to the woman's effective right to elect the procedure. Second is a confirmation of the State's power to restrict abortion after fetal viability, if the law contains exceptions for pregnancies which endanger a woman's life or health. And third is the principle that the State has legitimate interests

from the outset of the pregnancy in protecting the health of the woman and the life of the fetus that may become a child.[67]

In *Roe* the Court drew the line at viability based on a trimester framework; in *Casey* it upheld what it termed the "central holding" of *Roe*, but replaced the trimester framework with the undue-burden standard. By doing so, it rejected *Roe*'s finding that a woman had a fundamental right to abortion:

> In construing the phrase "liberty" incorporated in the Due Process Clause of the Fourteenth amendment, we have recognized that its meaning extends beyond freedom from physical restraint. . . . We are now of the view that, in terming this right fundamental, the Court in *Roe* read the earlier opinions upon which it based its decision much too broadly. Unlike marriage, procreation and conception, abortion "involves the purposeful termination of potential life. . . . The abortion decision must therefore be recognized as sui generis, different in kind from the others that the Court has protected under the rubric of personal or family privacy and autonomy" *[Harris v. McRae]*. . . . One cannot ignore the fact that a woman is not isolated in her pregnancy, and that the decision to abort necessarily involves the destruction of a fetus.[68]

Although women retained their rights to privacy and self-determination, as guaranteed by various amendments, the states gained constitutional sanction to enact restrictions that were rationally related to their interests. The split within the majority was over how to draw the boundary between women's rights and states' rights to regulate abortion, with three justices favoring the undue-burden standard and two supporting the trimester approach established in *Roe*.

The dissenters in *Casey* forcefully argued that by rejecting the notion of a fundamental right to abortion and the trimester framework protecting it, the majority had gutted *Roe* and left only its foundation standing: "*Roe* decided that a woman had a fundamental right to an abortion. The joint opinion rejects that view. *Roe* decided that abortion regulations were to be subject to 'strict scrutiny' and could be justified only in the light of 'compelling state interests.' The joint opinion rejects that view. . . . *Roe* analyzed abortion regulation under a rigid trimester framework, a framework which has guided the Court's decisionmaking for 19 years. The joint opinion rejects that framework."[69]

In upholding *Roe*, the plurality bridged this difference between itself and Justices Harry Blackmun and John Paul Stevens, who supported the trimester approach, by relying on *stare decisis* (the doctrine that previous judicial rulings will be followed unless they contravene the ordinary principles of justice): "Because neither the factual underpinnings of *Roe*'s central holding nor our understanding of it has changed (and because no other indication of weakened precedent has been shown) the Court could not pretend to be reexamining the prior law with any justification beyond a present doctrinal disposition to come out differently from the Court in 1973. To overrule prior law for no other reason than that would run counter to the view repeated in our cases, that a decision to overrule should rest on some special reason over and above the belief that a prior case was wrongly decided."[70]

In a dissent, Justice Antonin Scalia, joined by Rehnquist, White, and Clarence Thomas, dismissed this argument: "The Court's reliance upon *stare decisis* can best be described as contrived. It insists upon the necessity of adhering not at all to *Roe*, but only to what it calls the 'central holding.' It seems to me that *stare decisis* ought to be applied even to the doctrine of *stare decisis*, and I confess never to have heard of this new, keep-what-you-want-and-throw-away-the-rest version."[71]

In *Casey,* the Court ruled on specific provisions of the 1987 and 1989 Pennsylvania Abortion Control Acts and concluded that the informed-consent provision, a twenty-four-hour waiting period, the parental-consent requirement, and reporting requirements for physicians were constitutional, but that the spousal-consent requirement was not.[72] Since all these restrictions applied to the first trimester, *Casey* was a green light for other states to enact similarly restrictive legislation.[73]

The decision in *Casey* symbolized a legal and political revisiting of the pre-*Roe* period. As before, women seeking abortions encountered laws restricting their access to them; the role of the states was larger than it had been for twenty years. Activists on both sides mobilized, and abortion policy was front-page news again. To be sure, women in 1992 possessed a constitutional right to abortion that they had lacked twenty years earlier, but after two decades of conflict, it was no longer understood to be a fundamental right enshrined in the Constitution. That it remained by only a single vote demonstrated the enormous strides made by pro-life forces to restrict *Roe's* reach.

Notes

1. The precursor to the pro-life movement was the pro-family movement of the early 1970s, which favored school prayer and community involvement in textbook selection, and opposed busing and the teaching of homosexuality and evolution, which were believed to affect the integrity of the family unit. The pro-family movement was instrumental in defeating the equal-rights amendment by defining it and abortion as antifamily and antiwoman issues. By the late 1970s opponents of the equal-rights amendment had joined the emerging pro-life movement, which had briefly been aligned with the New Right. On the relationship

between abortion policy and the New Right, see Crawford 1980, Peele 1984, and Paige 1983.

2. This chapter is partly based on Nossiff 1995.

3. Some feminists opposed the term "choice," because it implied that all women had choices, whereas poor's women's choices were limited, and became more so after many states chose not to fund elective Medicaid abortions. On this point see, Condit 1990, p. 68.

4. The term "right-to-life" can be traced to a clause in the Declaration of Independence referring to the unalienable rights of "life, liberty, and the pursuit of happiness" (Shapiro 1972, pp. 10–11).

5. Title X of the Public Health Service Act (1970) gives grants to public and private organizations that provide family planning services.

6. *Webster v. Reproductive Health Services,* 109 S. Ct. 3034 (1989).

7. Lader 1973, p. 221.

8. Quoted in Luker 1984, p. 141.

9. *Eisenstadt v. Baird,* 405 U.S. 438 (1972).

10. *Roe v. Wade,* 410 U.S. at 159.

11. *Roe v. Wade,* at 162. It is possible to interpret these interests as separate, but it is more likely that Justice Harry Blackmun (author of the majority opinion) considered them to be two aspects of the same interest: the woman's health. In all its opinions in abortion cases in this period, the Court put the health of the pregnant woman and the right of physicians to practice medicine before states' rights to regulate access to abortions.

12. The significance of the Court's articulation of potential life as a state interest was initially brought home to me by one of my students, Leonore Crespo. It was not until the late 1970s, when it became necessary to create a broader rights paradigm incorporating the rights of the unborn as well as the state's rights to protect maternal health that pro-life supporters used this argument to their advantage.

13. *Doe v. Bolton,* 410 U.S. 179 (1973). This observation was made by Reagan (1997).

14. On *Doe v. Bolton,* see Rubin 1982.

15. "There remains, however, the required conformation by two Georgia-licensed physicians in addition to the recommendation of the pregnant woman's own consultant," the Court noted. Including the three physicians on the hospital's abortion committee, this meant that six physicians were involved in the abortion decision. "We conclude that this provision, too, must fall" (*Doe v. Bolton,* 410 U.S. 179 at 216).

16. Jain and Gooch 1972, p. 39.

17. *Doe v. Bolton* at 217.

18. Nolan 1983, p. 376.

19. See Craig and O'Brien 1993, Ch. 4.

20. Another leading state was Missouri, whose restrictive abortion laws were first challenged in 1976 with *Planned Parenthood of Central Missouri v. Danforth*, 428 U.S. 52 (1976). Challenges continued in the 1980s with *Planned Parenthood Association of Kansas City, Missouri v. Ashcroft*, 462 U.S. 476 (1983) and culminated in the 1989 decision in *Webster v. Reproductive Health Services*, 109 S. Ct. 3040 (1989), which signaled the beginning of a new era in post-*Roe* abortion policy. On Missouri, see Gorney 1998. On Massachusetts, see Borrelli 1995. Much of the basic information on post-*Roe* abortion politics in Pennsylvania is drawn from Halva-Neubauer 1992, Ch. 6.

21. Restrictions on public funding for poor women were upheld in *Maher v. Roe*, 432 U.S. 464 (1977) and *Poelker v. Doe*, 432 U.S. 59 (1977). On the federal level, Congress struggled with several variations of funding bans, beginning in 1974. For a discussion of the Hyde Amendment and other federal attempts to limit the use of public monies for abortion, see Craig and O'Brien 1993, Ch. 4.

22. The Senate passed the bill 42 to 5; the House passed it 146 to 41.

23. This view was expressed by Representative Robert Butera, house majority leader in 1974, in an interview, January 15, 1993. It agrees with the conclusion reached by abortion-repeal forces after introducing the second repeal bill in 1971.

24. Governors are limited to two terms in Pennsylvania. After *Roe*, realizing that pro-life forces in the state would continue to challenge him on abortion policy, Shapp concluded that it was more expedient to let the courts handle the issue than to squander his dwindling political support in his second term.

25. The veto was overridden by large margins in both the House (157 to 37) and the Senate (41 to 8).

26. *Planned Parenthood Association v. Fitzpatrick*, 401 F. Supp. 554 (E.D. PA 1975). For a discussion of Pennsylvania's role in crafting restrictive abortion law, see Nolan 1983, pp 380-81.

27. See discussion of *Colautti v. Franklin* below.

28. Nolan 1983, p. 381.

29. *Planned Parenthood of Central Missouri v. Danforth*, 428 U.S. 552, 49 L. Ed. 2d 788, 96 S. Ct 2831 (1976).

30. HCS House Bill No. 1211, Section 2 (2) (*Planned Parenthood of Central Missouri v. Danforth*, 428 U.S. 52, 49 L. Ed. 788, 96 S. Ct. 2831 at 813).

31. *Maher v. Roe*, 432 U.S. 464 (1977) and *Poelker v. Doe*, 432 U.S. 59 (1977).

32. *Colautti v. Franklin*, 439 U.S. 379 (1979). Section 5[a] of SB 1318 reads: "Protection of Life of Fetus.—[a] Every person who performs or induces an abortion shall prior thereto have made a determination based

on his experience, judgment or professional competence that the fetus is not viable, and if the determination is that *the fetus is viable or there is sufficient reason to believe that the fetus may be viable* [my italics], shall exercise that degree of professional skill, care and diligence to preserve the life and health of the fetus which such person would be required to exercise in order to preserve the life and health of any fetus intended to be born and not aborted and the abortion technique employed shall be that which would provide the best opportunity for the fetus to be aborted alive so long as a different technique would not be necessary in order to preserve or save the life of the mother."

33. *Colautti v. Franklin* at 604.

34. For the text of the human-life amendment supported by the National Right to Life Committee, which was created by the NCCB, see Frohock 1983, p. 114. For a detailed discussion of the NCCB's campaign, see Petchesky 1985 and Paige 1983.

35. Johnson and Bond 1980, pp. 185–207 and Hansen 1993, pp. 222–48.

36. See the results of the National Opinion Research Center Abortion Poll, 1974–1988, in *Public Opinion*, May/June 1987, p 37.

37. Rubin 1982, p. 138.

38. *City of Akron v. Akron Center for Reproductive Health*, 462 U.S. 416 (1983).

39. The suggestion that this standard be used was made by the Solicitor General, Brief Amicus Curiae of the United States in Support of Petitioners at 8, 18, *Akron* (No. 81-746) and *Ashcroft* (No. 81-1623), and by Justice O'Connor in her dissent in *Akron*. See also *Maher v. Roe*, 432 U.S. 464, 473, 53 L. Ed. 2d 484, 97 S. Ct. 2376 (1977), and *Harris v. McRae*, 448 U.S. 297, 314, 65 L. Ed. 2d 784, 100 S. Ct. (1980).

40. *Akron v. Akron Center for Reproductive Health*, at 718. For more discussion of this standard, see *Maher v. Roe*, *Bellotti v. Baird*, and *Harris v. McRae*.

41. *Planned Parenthood Association of Kansas City, Missouri v. Ashcroft*, 462 U.S. 476 (1983).

42. *Simopolous v. Virginia*, 462 U.S. 596 (1983). For an excellent discussion of the significance of this trio of abortion cases, see Fox 1983. For a description of the definition of "hospital" provided by the Virginia Legislature, see Fox p. 149, n. 104. See also Fox's discussion of the hospital requirement (pp. 151–52).

43. Ibid., p. 156.

44. Ibid., pp. 156–57.

45. For an interesting discussion of the relationship between the Court's deference to the medical profession and its view of women's rights in abortion cases, see *Harvard Law Review*, Vol. 97 (1983): 70–86.

46. Halva-Neubauer 1992, p. 295. This trend was also evident in the organization of grassroots groups. In Pennsylvania, the PCC's control over abortion policy was weakened by the emergence of independent grassroots organizations such as the Pennsylvania Pro-Life Federation, which were often aligned with national organizations and were able to adopt a more pragmatic approach to abortion policy than the Catholic Conference.

47. Martin Mullen, the chief legislative leader for HB 800 and SB 1318, lost his seat as a result of redistricting. Mullen's passionate style and moral approach to abortion policy worked well in the 1970s, while the Catholic Conferences retained the upper hand on the state level, but it was less effective as pro-life forces attained national prominence. That the pro-life legislative campaign was taken over by two Republican legislators in the 1980s was another indication of the ascendancy of individual pro-life legislators and the declining importance of parties in the abortion war on the state level.

48. For a complete list, see Halva-Neubauer 1992, pp. 275, 297–99.

49. Ibid.

50. Nolan 1983, pp. 396-98.

51. The requirement that the Department of Health provide pictures of fetal development as part of the informed-consent provision was deleted. Also deleted in the final version of the bill was language asserting that life began at conception (Nolan 1983, pp. 382–83; Halva-Neubauer 1992, p. 304). The parental-consent provision of the 1982 act was addressed in *American College of Obstetrics and Gynecologists v. Thornburgh*, 737 F.2d 283 (1984), where the Court ruled it should remain enjoined until the Pennsylvania Supreme Court could write rules to protect the confidentiality of minors. See *Thornburgh* at 397.

52. *H.L. v. Matheson* 450 U.S. 398 (1981), *Danforth, Ashcroft,* and *Simpolous.*

53. In a wrongful birth suit persons seek damages for the failure of the defendant to order tests that would have indicated the fetus was likely to be deformed. In a wrongful life suit, a person with a deformity would sue and claim that he/she should not have been born. Both measures were added with the intention of decreasing the number of abortions. See Halva-Neubauer 1992, pp. 297–98 and 308.

54. *Thornburgh v. American College of Obstetricians & Gynecologists*, 476 U.S. 747 90 L. Ed. 2d 779, 106 S. Ct. 2169. (1986).

55. For a detailed analysis of the legal precedents of each restriction, see James J. Knicely 1986.

56. See Knicely 1986, pp. 278–83.

57. *Thornburgh* at 793.

58. *Thornburgh* at 817.

59. *Harvard Law Review,* Vol. 100: 200–210. This citation, p 201.

60. This discussion of the 1987 Abortion Control Act is based on Halva-Neubauer 1992, Ch. 6, especially pp. 313–26. For a complete list of the provisions of the 1987 Abortion Control Act, see ibid., pp. 314–15.

61. Like his predecessors, the newly elected governor, Robert Casey, did not wish to squander his political credit on a bill that he considered likely to be overturned. He vetoed the 1987 bill, determining that the physician-reporting and paternal-notification requirements were still outside the constitutional limits established by the Supreme Court. Several months later, however, his office drafted the 1988 Abortion Control Act, which was similar to the 1987 version but omitted the paternal-consent provision. As expected, the 1988 act was challenged in court, but full consideration of it was delayed by the states pending the outcome of *Webster.*

62. See Craig and O'Brien 1993, pp. 86, 95. The issue of where abortions are performed has also limited women's access to abortions, given the decreasing numbers of abortion providers and the prohibitions that several states have placed on public hospitals performing them.

63. For a thorough discussion of restrictions on abortion on the state level, see Rosenberg 1991, pp. 187–93. Rosenberg 1991, pp. 188–93.

64. *Rust v. Sullivan,* 111 S. Ct. (1991). This shift was particularly evident two years later in the *Rust v. Sullivan* decision, where the Supreme Court ruled that regulations enacted by Congress banning abortion counseling in family-planning clinics receiving federal funds did not infringe on the First Amendment rights of doctors or patients seeking abortions.

65. Quoted in Gorney 1992, p. 22.

66. *Planned Parenthood of Southeastern Pennsylvania v. Casey,* 112 S.Ct. 2791 [1192] 120 L. Ed. 2d, at 674.

67. *Casey* at 694.

68. *Casey* at 763–64.

69. *Casey* at 765.

70. *Casey* at 706.

71. *Casey* at 791.

72. The parental-consent provision, which was also upheld in *Casey,* had been included in the 1974 Abortion Control Act, but its implementation had been delayed for twenty years by a series of legal challenges.

73. For a discussion of post-*Casey* legislation in other states, see Craig and O'Brien 1993, pp. 348–49.

Conclusion

With the 1973 decision in *Roe v. Wade,* pro-abortion activists succeeded in securing women's rights to early abortions with limited state interference. But *Roe* did not settle the issue. After 1973, abortion policy became a national issue, and the next twenty-five years saw a passionate struggle between supporters and opponents of the right to abortion. The conflict affected all levels and branches of government and both political parties, and spawned two social movements. It was also the catalyst for the formation of innumerable interest groups and political-action committees.

In the 1980s, after a decade of pro-life marches and sit-ins at clinics, the conflict became more violent, with abortion clinics being bombed and staff members being stalked and threatened. In the 1990s the violence escalated again, with the killing of doctors and staff members at several clinics around the country.[1] The range of reasons for this ongoing controversy can be traced to three fundamental factors discussed in this book.

First was the emergence of women as a political constituency in the 1960s, a time of expanding grassroots participation and judicial activism. The mobilization of women began during the Kennedy administration around issues of equal opportunity. By 1965, when abortion activists on the state level began organizing to change the laws, a tiny network of politically experienced women had emerged. A year later some of them founded the National Organization for

Women. The abortion issue expanded this network because it affected women's lives in a direct way. Feminists from NOW and radical women's-liberation groups aligned and formed a feminist-discourse coalition that pressed for the repeal of existing abortion laws. The issue of abortion also served to mobilize women opposed to the feminist agenda. After *Roe,* many women who had not been politically active joined the pro-life movement as well as campaigns to stop the ratification of the equal rights amendment.

The second factor was the American political system, in terms of both the power of the judicial branch and its federalist structure, which provided institutional access to groups on both sides of the debate. The broader application of the Fourteenth Amendment by the federal courts in the 1960s complemented the efforts of pro-abortion activists to portray restrictive abortion laws as infringements of women's rights to privacy and liberty. The procedural changes initiated by the courts increased the activists' access to the legal process.

With its 1965 decision in *Griswold v. Connecticut,* the Court laid the foundation for a national reproductive policy based on privacy. The 1969 decisions in *United States v. Vuitch* and *People v. Belous* encouraged suits in other states, increasing pressure on the courts. These legal developments were particularly beneficial to pro-abortion activists because their chief resource in challenging restrictive abortion laws was a rights-based argument, which was better suited to the legal arena than to the court of public opinion.

Antiabortion forces retaliated in the legislatures. By framing their demands in terms of states' rights to protect fetal life, and by employing a religious discourse that equated abortion with murder, they defined the debate in moral terms that resonated on the grassroots level. The numerous points of access provided by a federalist system of government expanded the scope of the conflict. This benefited pro-life forces in the post-*Roe* period because it helped them to generate support on the state and local level and to persuade legislators to enact restrictions favored by the majority of people.

The case studies of New York and Pennsylvania illustrate how these developments came together before *Roe*. The outcomes of the postwar reform movements in the 1950s affected the two states' party systems in different ways in the following decade. The comparatively open party system in New York, when combined with interest-group politics and feminist participation, led to the 1970 passage of the repeal bill. Pennsylvania's closed party system, coupled with the PCC's mobilization and the limited participation of groups in favor of reform, resulted in the adoption of a highly restrictive abortion bill in 1972.

The third factor was the *Roe* decision itself. Although the decision ran counter to the views of the majority of people at the time, who favored laws legalizing therapeutic abortions, as opposed to the repeal of restrictions on first-trimester abortions, majorities since 1973 have supported *Roe*'s chief finding: that early access to abortion should be constitutionally protected.[2] By articulating states' interests in protecting potential life alongside women's rights to privacy and liberty, the Court's decision ignited the conflict over abortion by providing the neophyte pro-life movement with a powerful rights paradigm based on potential life and state interests. The stage was set for a contest between opposing forces to fix the point of viability. As a result, the main conflict centered on the unanswerable questions of when life begins and when the state's interests come into play. Had the Court assigned the regulation of abortions to licensed physicians, the medical interest of the states would have been protected without their further involvement, in large part defusing the controversy.[3]

Pennsylvania's passage of the 1974 Abortion Control Act paved the way for other states: By 1975, thirty-two states had adopted restrictive abortion laws.[4] In addition, several states, including Missouri and Rhode Island, passed fetal-protection statutes based on the assumption that life began at conception; under this assumption, laws designed to protect the embryo would be constitutional.[5] In its 1976 decision in *Danforth*, its first major decision on abortion policy after *Roe*, the Supreme Court retreated by upholding first-trimester restrictions. This provided pro-life activists with the opportunity to chip away at *Roe*'s boundaries. Had the Supreme Court held firm to its decision in *Roe*, the debate over abortion policy might have been gradually contained.

In the mid-1970s, pro-life forces aligned themselves with conservative Republicans who were opposed to elective abortions. As a result, when Ronald Reagan was elected in 1980, they were well placed to benefit from his administration's support of restrictive abortion policy, which seemed to mirror the sentiment in the country for limiting access to abortions in certain circumstances.[6]

The Supreme Court's 1983 decisions on abortion cases foreshadowed the emergence of significant changes in its approach to restrictive laws. Although the Court struck down several abortion restrictions in its decision in *Akron*, Sandra Day O'Connor based her dissent on an "undue burden" standard, which later replaced *Roe*'s trimester framework. Despite or because of these decisions, there was a dramatic increase in violence against clinics the following year, which suggested that factions within the pro-life movement were dissatisfied with what they considered to be incremental gains. In 1984, there were 132 incidents against abortion clinics, compared with a total of 149 reported from 1977 through 1983.[7] The number of disruptive acts in 1984, including hate mail, phone calls, bomb threats, and picketing, jumped to 209, from 125 for 1977 through 1983.

Pro-choice groups responded with lawsuits, while national pro-life groups staged blockades at clinics across the country. Chief among these groups was Operation Rescue, which gained national attention by successfully closing down abortion clinics in Atlanta during the 1988 Democratic National Convention. In that year 182 incidents were reported at clinic blockades, as opposed to two such incidents the year before.

Throughout the 1980s, leading pro-life states such as Pennsylvania and Missouri continued to pass comprehensive abortion acts aimed at further restricting abortion access. Although the Supreme Court struck down the main provision of Pennsylvania's 1982 act, in *Casey* it upheld similar kinds of restrictions governing first-trimester abortions that pro-life forces in Pennsylvania had been proposing for decades.

Thirty-five years after *Griswold,* the debate over abortion policy remains unresolved. Pro-choice supporters argue that *Roe* protects women's individual rights to life, liberty, and property; pro-lifers argue that it violates the same rights of the unborn. In terms of these competing rights, no compromise is possible. This is the fundamental and unresolvable paradox underlying abortion policy in America. The future of the issue lies between the ability of pro-life forces to enact more restrictions within the parameters established by *Webster* and *Casey,* and the ability of pro-choice supporters to use the arguments established by *Roe* to stop them.

Notes

1. National Abortion Federation Fact Sheet, January 1999.

2. Although there is some disagreement on how to interpret the polls, a tabulation of the National Opinion Research Center's results from 1974 to 1991 indicates that a high majority of Americans have supported abortion in "hard" cases (rape, incest, fetal deformity, or danger to the woman's life) since the 1960s. Support for abortion in "soft" cases (personal choice, economic hardship) has stayed around 50 percent. This is one reason that there has been majority support for restrictions on abortions (*Public Opinion*, May-June 1989; Craig and O'Brien 1993, pp. 252–54; Wetstein 1996, p. 64).

3. Based on the pre-*Roe* pattern, some have argued that had the Court simply declared the Texas statute unconstitutional and not gone on to fashion a national abortion policy, the states would have continued to pass reform laws that were supported by most people at the time. Such a decision, however, would merely have perpetuated the unequal access women had to abortion. Without the decision, a few more states would have either reformed or repealed their statutes (four states had repealed their laws before *Roe*), but the majority would have retained laws that prohibited all abortions except when the woman's life was endangered (Nossiff 1994b).

4. Rubin 1982, p. 127.

5. Ibid., p. 130.

6. *Public Opinion*, May-June 1989: 37.

7. National Abortion Federation Fact Sheet, January 1999.

References

Abbott, Walter, ed. 1966. *The Documents of Vatican II*. New York: Herder and Herder.

"Abortion Issue Spurs Battle as Pennsylvania Democrats Adopt Platform." 1970. *Philadelphia Daily News*, September 15, p. 26.

Ad-Hoc Committee for SB 1318. 1974. August 8, pp. 2–4, Harrisburg, Pa.

Andrain, Charles F., and David E. Apter. 1966. *Political Protests and Social Change: Analyzing Politics*. New York: New York University Press.

Association for the Study of Abortion. 1966. *Headquarters Report*. New York, N.Y.

Baehr, Ninia. 1990. *Abortion Without Apology: A Radical History for the 1990s*. Pamphlet No. 8. Boston: South End Press, 1990.

Banfield, Edward C. 1965. *Big City Politics*. Cambridge, Mass.: Harvard University Press.

Banfield, Edward C., and James Q. Wilson. 1963. *City Politics*. Cambridge, Mass.: Harvard University Press.

Baumgartner, Frank F., and Bryan D. Jones. 1993. *Agendas and Instability in American Politics*. Chicago: University of Chicago Press.

Beers, Paul B. 1980. *Pennsylvania Politics Today and Yesterday: The Tolerable Accommodation*. University Park, Pa.: The Pennsylvania State University Press.

Benestad, J. Brian, and Francis J. Butler, eds. 1981. *Quest for Justice: A Compendium of Statements of the United States Catholic Bishops on the Political and Social Order, 1966–1980*. Washington, D.C.: United States Catholic Conference.

"Bishops' Statement Urges Veto Override." 1974. *The Catholic Standard and Times* (Philadelphia, Pa.), September 5, p. 1.

"Bishop to Fight Abortion Bill." 1970. *The Morning Call* (Allentown, Pa.), August 23, p. 23.

Black, Forrest L. 1970. "Abortions Become Election Issue." *The Evening Bulletin* (Pittsburgh, Pa.), September 23, p. 1.

Blake, Judith. 1971. "Abortion and Public Opinion: The 1960–1970 Decade." *Science* 171 (February 12): 540–49.

———. 1977. "The Abortion Decisions: Judicial Review and Public Opinion." Pp. 51–83 in *Abortion: New Directions for Policy Studies*, edited by

Edward Manier, William Liu, and David Solomon. Notre Dame, Ind.: University of Notre Dame Press.

Borrelli, Mary Anne. 1995. "Abortion Policy in Transition." Pp. 182–204 in *Abortion Politics in American States,* edited by Mary C. Segers and Timothy A. Byrnes. Armonk, N.Y.: M.E. Sharpe.

Browning, Rufus, Dale Rogers Marshall, and David H. Tabb, eds. 1990. *Racial Politics in American Cities.* New York: Longman.

Brutto, Carmen. 1972a. "House Bid to Override Abortion Bill Fails." *The Patriot* (Harrisburg, Pa.), December 1, p. 1.

———. 1972b. "House Presented 2 Abotion Bills." *The Patriot* (Harrisburg, Pa.), June 16, p. 15.

———. 1972c. "House Alters Bill to Ban Abortions." *The Patriot* (Harrisburg, Pa.), June 21, p. 1.

Byrnes, Timothy A. 1991. *Catholic Bishops in American Politics.* Princeton, N.J.: Princeton University Press.

Byrnes, Timothy A., and Mary Segers, eds. 1992. *The Catholic Church and The Politics of Abortion: A View from the States.* Boulder, Col.: Westview Press.

Carabillo, Judith Meuli, and June Bundy Csiad. 1993. *Feminist Chronicles.* Los Angeles: Women's Graphics. Pp. 161–62.

Carden, Maren Lockwood. 1977. *Feminism in the Mid-1970s.* New York: Ford Foundation.

Carmen, Arlene, and Howard Moody. 1973. *Abortion Counseling and Social Change: From Illegal Act to Medical Practice.* Valley Forge, Pa.: Judson Press.

Chaffe, William. 1972. *The American Woman: Her Changing Social, Economic, and Political Roles.* New York: Oxford University Press.

"Churches Affirm Stand on Abortion." 1970. *The Morning Call* (Allentown, Pa.), October 7, p. 16.

Cisler, Lucinda. 1970. "Unfinished Business: Birth Control." Pp. 254–89 in *Sisterhood is Powerful,* edited by Robin Morgan. New York: Vintage.

Clark, Tom C. 1969. "Religion, Morality, and Abortion: A Constitutional Appraisal." *Loyola University Law Review* 2: 8–9.

Cobb, Roger, and Charles Elder. 1972. *Participation in American Politics: The Dynamics of Agenda-Building.* Boston: Allyn and Bacon.

The Committee for the Cook-Leicher Bill. 1970. *Chronicle of the Activities.* May. New York, N.Y.

Condit, Celeste Michelle. 1990. *Decoding Abortion Rhetoric: Communicating Social Change.* Illinois: University of Illinois Press.

Cooney, John. 1984. *The American Pope: The Life and Times of Francis Cardinal Spellman.* New York: Times Books.

Costain, Anne N. 1992. *Inviting Women's Rebellion: A Political Process Interpretation of the Women's Movement.* Baltimore: The Johns Hopkins University Press.

Craig, Barbara Hinkson, and David M. O'Brien. 1993. *Abortion and American Politics.* Chatham, N.J.: Chatham House.

Crawford, Alan. 1980. *Thunder On the Right: The "New Right" and the Politics of Resentment.* New York: Pantheon Books.

Critchlow, Donald T. 1999. *Intended Consequences: Birth Control, Abortion, and the Federal Government in Modern America.* New York: Oxford University Press.

Critchlow, Paul. 1974. "Abortion Bill Voted by House." *Philadelphia Inquirer,* July 11, p. 1.

Crumlish, Joseph D. 1959. *A City Finds Itself: The Philadelphia Home Rule Charter Movement.* Detroit: Wayne State University Press.

Deckard, Barbara S. 1983. *The Women's Movement.* 3rd ed. New York: Harper.

Diani, Mario. 1996. "Linking Mobilization Frames and Political Opportunities: Insights from Regional Populism in Italy." *American Sociological Review* 61 (December): 1053–69.

Dienes, C. Thomas. 1972. *Law, Politics, and Birth Control.* Urbana: University of Illinois Press.

Diesling, Paul. 1962. *Five Types of Decisions and Their Social Conditions.* Urbana: University of Illinois Press.

Dodd, Lawrence C., and Calvin Jillson, eds. 1994. *The Dynamics of American Politics: Approaches and Interpretations.* Boulder, Col.: Westview.

Drinan, Robert F. 1967. "Strategy on Abortion." *America* 116 (February 4): 177–79.

Dugan, George. 1967. "State's 8 Catholic Bishops Ask Fight on Abortion Bill; Pastoral Letter Read." *The New York Times,* February 13, p. A1.

East, Catherine. 1983. "Newer Commissions." In *Women in Washington,* edited by Irene Tinker. New York: Sage Publications.

Ebaugh, Helen Rose Fuchs, and C. Allen Haney. 1980. "Shifts in Abortion Attitudes, 1972–1978." *Journal of Marriage and the Family* 42: 491–99.

Ecanbarger, William. 1972a. "Mullen Assails Governor." *Philadelphia Inquirer,* December 1, p. 1.

———.1972b. "Senate Votes to Ban Nearly All Abortions, Sends Bill to House." *Philadelphia Inquirer,* December 1, p. 1.

———. 1974. "Veto Refused; Abortion Bill Becomes Law." *Philadelphia Inquirer,* September 11, p. 1.

Echols, Alice. 1989. *Daring To be Bad: Radical Feminism in America, 1967–1975.* Minneapolis: University of Minnesota Press.

Edelman, Murray. 1971. *Politics as Symbolic Action: Mass Arousal and Quiescence.* New York: Academic Press.

Eisinger, Peter. 1973. "The Conditions of Protest Behavior in American Cities." *American Political Science Review* 67: 11–28.

Emerson, Thomas I. 1965. "Nine Justices in Search of a Doctrine." *Michigan Law Review* 64: 219–34.

Faux, Marion. 1988. Roe v. Wade: *The Untold Story of The Landmark Supreme Court Decision That Made Abortion Legal.* New York: Penguin.

Ferris, Abbott L. 1971. *Indicators of Trends in the Status of Women.* New York: Russell Sage Foundation.

Finkbine, Sherri. 1967. "The Lesser of Two Evils." In *The Case for Legalized Abortion Now,* edited by Alan F. Guttmacher. Berkeley, Calif.: Diablo Press.

Fox, Laura. "The 1983 Abortion Decisions: Clarification of the Permissible Limits on Abortion Regulation." *University of Richmond Law Review* 18: 137–59.

Foy, Felicia A. 1971. *1971 Catholic Almanac.* Paterson, N.J.: Saint Anthony's Guild.

Francome, Colin. 1984. *Abortion Freedom.* London: George Allen & Unwin.

Freedman, Robert L. 1963. *A Report on Politics in Philadelphia.* Cambridge, Mass.: The Joint Center for Urban Studies, M.I.T./Harvard.

Freeman, Jo. 1975. *The Politics of Women's Liberation.* New York: David McKay.

———, ed. 1983 "On the Origins of Social Movements." In *Social Movements of the Sixties and Seventies.* New York: Longman Press.

Friedan, Betty. 1963. *The Feminine Mystique.* New York: W.W. Norton.

———. 1985. *It Changed My Life: Writings on the Women's Movement.* New York: W.W. Norton.

Frohock, Fred M. 1983. *Abortion: A Case Study in Law and Morals.* Westport, Conn.: Greenwood Press.

Garrow, David J. 1994. *Liberty and Sexuality: The Right to Privacy and the Making of* Roe v. Wade. New York: Maxwell Macmillan International.

Gebhard, Paul, Wardell B. Pomeroy, Clyde E. Martin, and Cornellia V. Christenson, eds. 1958. *Pregnancy, Birth, and Abortion.* New York: Harper & Brothers and Paul E. Hoeber.

Gelb, Joyce, and Marian Palley. 1987. *Women and Public Policies.* 2nd ed. Princeton, N.J.: Princeton University Press.

George, B. James, Jr. 1973. "The Evolving Law on Abortion." In *Abortion, Society, and the Law,* edited by David F. Walbert and J. Douglas Butler. Cleveland: Case Western University Press.

Ginsburg, Faye D. 1989. *Contested Lives: The Abortion Debate in an American Community.* Berkeley: University of California Press.

Goffman, Erving. 1981. *Forms of Talk*. Philadelphia: University of Pennsylvania Press.

Gorney, Cynthia. 1992. "Endgame." *The Washington Post Magazine*, February 23.

———. 1998. *Articles of Faith: A Frontline History of the Abortion Wars*. New York: Simon & Schuster.

Hajer, Maarten A. 1993. "Discourse Coalitions and the Institutionalization of Practice: The Case of Acid Rain in Britain." Pp. 43–76 in *The Argumentative Turn in Policy Analysis and Planning*, edited by Frank Fischer and John Forestor. Durham, N.C.: Duke University Press.

———. 1995. *The Politics of Environmental Discourse*. Oxford: Oxford University Press.

Halva-Neubauer, Glen Arlen. 1992. "Legislative Agenda Setting in the States: The Case of Abortion Policy." Ph.D. dissertation, University of Minnesota.

Hansen, Susan B. 1980. "State Implementation of Supreme Court Decisions: Abortion Rates Since *Roe v. Wade*." *The Journal of Politics* 42: 372–95.

———. 1993. "State Differences in Abortion Rates: Electoral and Policy Context." In *Understanding the New Politics of Abortion*, edited by Malcom Goggin. Beverly Hills, Calif.: Sage Publications.

Harrison, Beverly Wilding. 1983. *Our Rights to Choose: Toward A New Ethic of Abortion*. Boston: Beacon Press.

Hertzke, Allen D. 1988. *Representing God in Washington: The Role of Religious Lobbies in the American Polity*. Knoxville: The University of Tennessee Press.

Hickling, Cathy. 1978. "Pro-Life Veteran Mary Winter Keeps Pressing on After 18 Years of Activism." *Expression* (January), p. 10.

Hole, Judith, and Ellen Levine. 1971. *Rebirth of Feminism*. New York: Quadrangle Books.

Jain, Sagar C., and Laurel Gooch. 1972. *Georgia Abortion Act, 1968: A Study in Legislative Process*. Chapel Hill: University of North Carolina, School of Public Health.

Jain, Sagar C., and Steven Hughes. 1969. *California Abortion Act, 1967: A Study in Legislative Process*. Chapel Hill: University of North Carolina, Carolina Population Center.

Jain, Sagar C., and Steven W. Sinding. 1968. *North Carolina Abortion Law 1967: A Study in Legislative Process*. Chapel Hill: University of North Carolina Press.

Johnson, Charles A., and John R. Bond. 1980. "Coercive and Noncoercive Abortion Deterrence Policies." In *Policy Implementation: Penalties of Incentives?* edited by J. Brigham and D. W. Brown. Beverly Hills, Calif.: Sage.

Judd, Dennis R., 1988. *The Politics of American Cities: Private Power and Public Policy.* Glenview, Ill.: Scott, Foresman and Company.

Keiser, Richard A. 1990. "The Rise of a Biracial Coalition in Philadelphia." Pp. 49–74 in *Racial Politics in American Cities,* edited by Rufus P. Browning, Dale Roger Marshall, and David H. Tabb. New York: Longman.

Kifner, John. 1968. "Abortion Reform Dies in Assembly." *The New York Times,* April 4, p. 1.

Kingdon, John W. 1984. *Agendas, Alternatives and Public Policies.* Boston: Little, Brown.

Kirp, David L. 1982. "Professionalization as Policy Choice: British Special Education in Comparative Perspective." *World Politics:* 137–74.

Kitschelt, Herbert P. 1986. "Political Opportunity Structures and Political Protest: Anti-Nuclear Movements in Four Democracies," *British Journal of Political Science* 16: 57–85.

Klein, Ethel. 1984. *Gender Politics.* Cambridge, Mass.: Harvard University Press.

Knicely, James J. 1986. "The *Thornburgh and Bowers Cases: Consequences for* Roe v. Wade. *Mississippi Law Journal* 56: 267–323.

Kriesi, Hanspeter, et al. 1995. *New Social Movements in Western Europe: A Comparative Analysis.* Minneapolis: University of Minnesota Press.

Lader, Lawrence. 1973. *Abortion II: Making the Revolution.* Boston: Beacon Press.

"Liberalized Bill on Abortion Fails, But House Balks at Outright Ban." 1972. *Philadelphia Inquirer,* June 21, p. 1.

Littlewood, Thomas B. 1977. *The Politics of Population Control.* Notre Dame, Ind.: University of Notre Dame Press.

Lowi, Theodore J. 1964. *At the Pleasure of the Mayor: Patronage and Power in New York City, 1891–1958.* London: The Free Press of Glencoe.

———. 1988. "Foreword: New Dimensions in Policy and Politics." Pp. x–xxi in *Social Regulatory Policy: Moral Controversies in American Politics,* edited byRaymond Tatalovich and Byron W. Daynes. Boulder, Col: Westview Press.

Lucas, Roy. 1968. "Federal Constitutional Limitations on the Enforcement and Administration of State Abortion Statutes." *North Carolina Law Review* 46: 730–78.

Luker, Kristin. 1984. *Abortion & The Politics of Motherhood.* Berkeley: University of California Press.

Lynch, Dan. 1972. "Why an Anti-Abortion Law? It Was Easier," *Philadelphia Inquirer,* November 26, p. 3-H.

Mansbridge, Jane J. 1986. *Why We Lost the ERA.* Chicago: University of Chicago Press.

Mayhew, David R. 1986. *Placing Parties in American Politics*. Princeton, N.J.: Princeton University Press.

McAdam, Doug. 1982. *Political Process and the Development of Black Insurgency*. Chicago: University of Chicago Press.

Means, Cyril. 1968. "The Law of New York Concerning Abortion and the State of the Foetus, 1664–1968: A Case of Cessation and Constitutionality." *New York Law Forum* 14.

———. 1971. "The Phoenix of Abortional Freedom: Is a Penumbral or Ninth Amendment Right About to Arise From the Nineteenth-Century Legislative Ashes of a Fourteenth-Century Common Law Liberty?" *New York Forum* 17: 335–410.

Merton, Andrew. 1981. *Enemies of Choice*. Boston: Beacon Press.

Mohr, James C. 1973. *The Radical Republicans and Reform in New York During Reconstruction*. Ithaca, N.Y.: Cornell University Press.

———. 1978. *Abortion in America: The Origins and Evolution of National Policy, 1800–1900*. New York: Oxford University Press.

Mooney, Christopher Z., and Mei-Hsien Lee. 1995. "Legislative Morality in the American States: The Case of Pre-*Roe* Abortion Regulation Reform." *American Journal of Political Science* 39 (3): 599–627.

Morgan, Richard E. 1968. *The Politics of Religious Conflict: Church and State in America*. New York: Pegasus.

Morgan, Robin, ed. 1970. *Sisterhood Is Powerful*. New York: Vintage.

Neier, Aryeh. 1992. *Only Judgment*. Middletown, Conn.: Wesleyan University Press.

Nolan, Nancy. 1983. "Toward Constitutional Abortion Control Legislation: The Pennsylvania Approach." *Dickinson Law Review* 87: 376–406.

New Yorkers for Abortion Law Repeal. 1969. *Newsletter,* April 2 and June 13. New York, N.Y.

Noonan, John T., Jr. 1970. "An Almost Absolute Value in History." In *The Morality of Abortion,* edited by John T. Noonan, Jr. Cambridge, Mass: Harvard University Press.

Nossiff, Rosemary. 1994a. "Abortion Policy in New York and Pennsylvania, 1965–1972." Ph.D. dissertation., Cornell University.

———. 1994b. "Why Justice Ginsburg Is Wrong About States Expanding Abortion Rights." *Political Science* (June), pp. 227–31.

———. 1995. "Pennsylvania: The Impact of Party Organization and Religious Lobbying." Pp. 16–27 in *Abortion Politics in American States,* edited by Mary C. Segers and Timothy A. Byrnes. Armonk, N.Y.: M.E. Sharpe.

———. 1998. "Discourse, Party, and Policy: The Case of Abortion." *Policy Studies Journal* 26 (2): 244–56.

Orren, Karen, and Stephen Skowroneck. 1994. "Beyond the Iconography of Order: Notes for a 'New Institutionalism.'" In *The Dynamics of American Politics: Approaches and Interpretations,* edited by Lawrence C. Dodd and Calvin Jillson. Boulder, Col.: Westview Press.

Paige, Connie. 1983. *The Right To Lifers: Who They Are, How They Operate, Where They Get Their Money.* New York: Summit Books.

Peele, Gillian. 1984. *Revival and Reaction: The Right in Contemporary America.* Oxford: Oxford University Press.

Pennsylvania Abortion Coalition. 1972. *Newsletter* 1 (3). Pittsburgh, Pa.

Pennsylvanians in Support of House Bill 536. *Newsletter* 2. Pittsburgh, Pa.

People Concerned for the Unborn Child. 1974. *Newsletter* 2 (9). Pittsburgh, Pa.

Petchesky, Rosalind Pollack. 1984. *Abortion and Woman's Choice: The State, Sexuality, and Reproductive Freedom.* Boston: Northeastern University Press.

Petshek, Kirk R. 1973. *The Challenge of Urban Reform.* Philadelphia: Temple University Press.

Philadelphia Women's Political Caucus. 1974. *Newsletter* 3 (5). Philadelphia, Pa.

Piven, Francis Fox, and Richard A. Cloward. 1977. *Poor People's Movements: Why They Succeed, How They Fail.* New York: Pantheon Books.

"The Proper Response." 1974. *The Evening Bulletin* (Philadelphia, Pa.), July 17, p. 42.

Reagan, Leslie R. 1997. *When Abortion Was a Crime: Women, Law, and Medicine in the United States, 1867–1973.* Berkeley: University of California Press.

Redlich, Norman D. 1962. "Are There Certain Rights . . . Retained by the People?" *New York Law Review* 37: 787–812.

Reed, James. 1978. *The Birth Control Movement and American Society: From Private Vice to Public Virtue.* Princeton, N.J.: Princeton University Press.

Reichley, James. 1959. *The Art of Government: Reform and Organization Politics in Philadelphia.* New York: The Fund for the Republic.

Rosen, Harold, ed. 1954. *Therapeutic Abortion: Medical, Psychiatric, Legal, Anthropological and Religious Considerations.* New York: Julian Press.

Rosenberg, Gerald N. 1991. *The Hollow Hope: Can Courts Bring About Social Change?* Chicago: University of Chicago Press.

Rubin, Eva R. 1982. *Abortion, Politics, and the Courts:* Roe v. Wade *and Its Aftermath.* Westport, Conn.: Greenwood Press.

―――. 1987. *Abortion, Politics, and the Courts.* Revised edition. Westport, Conn.: Greenwood Press.

Russell, Keith. 1951. "Therapeutic Abortion in a General Hospital." *American Journal of Obstetrics and Gynecology* 62: 434–38.

Ryan, Barbara. 1992. *Feminism and the Women's Movement: Dynamics of Change in Social Movement Ideology and Activism.* New York: Routledge.

Sarat, Austin. 1982. "Abortion and the Courts: Uncertain Boundaries of Law and Politics." Pp. 113–51 in *American Politics and Public Policy,* edited by Allan P. Sindler. Washington, D.C.: CQ Press.

Sarvis, Betty, and Hyman Rodman. 1974. *The Abortion Controversy,* 2nd ed. New York: Columbia University Press.

Schambelan, Bo. 1992. Roe v. Wade: *The Complete Text of the Official U.S. Supreme Court Decision.* Philadelphia: Running Press.

Schanberg, Sydney H. 1967. "State's 8 Catholic Bishops Ask Fight on Abortion Bill: Bill's Backer Loses Post." *New York Times,* February 13, p. A1

———. 1968. "Rockefeller Asks Abortion Reform." *The New York Times,* January 10, p. A-23.

Schattschneider, E. E. 1960. *The Semi-Sovereign People.* New York: Holt, Rinehart and Winston.

Shapiro, Fred C. 1972. "Right to Life Has a Message for New York State Legislature." *New York Times Magazine,* August 20.

"Shapp Vetoes Strict Abortion Control." 1974. *The Patriot* (Harrisburg, Pa.), July 13, p. 2.

Shefter, Martin. 1983. "Regional Receptivity to Reform," *Political Science Quarterly* 98: 459–83.

———. 1985. *Political Crisis/Fiscal Crisis: The Collapse and Revival of New York City.* New York: Basic Books.

———. 1988. "The Electoral Framework." Pp. 151–78 in *The Two New Yorks: State-City Relations in the Changing Federal System,* edited by Gerald Benjamin and Charles Brecher. New York: Russell Sage Foundation.

Sigworth, Heather. 1971. "Abortion Laws in the Federal Courts: The Supreme Court as Platonic Guardian." *Indiana Legal Forum* 5 (Fall): 130–42.

Silverberg, Helene N. 1988. "Political Organization and the Origin of Identity: The Emergence and Containment of Gender in American Politics, 1960–1984." Ph.D. dissertation, Cornell University.

Silverstein, Mark, and Benjamin Ginsberg. 1987. "The Supreme Court and the New Politics of Judicial Power." *Political Science Quarterly* 102 (Fall): 371–88.

Snow, David A, E. Burke Rochford Jr, Steven K. Worden, and Robert D. Benford. 1986. "Frame Alignment Processes, Micromobilization, and Movement Participation." *American Sociological Review* 51 (August): 464–81.

Sorauf, Frank J. 1963. *Party and Representation: Legislative Politics in Pennsylvania.* New York: Prentice Hall.

Staggenborg, Suzanne. 1991. *The Pro-Choice Movement: Organization and Activism in the Abortion Conflict.* New York: Oxford University Press.

"State House Unit Clears 2 Bills on Abortion—One Pro, One Con." 1972. *Philadelphia Inquirer,* June 15, p. 4.

Stave, Bruce M. 1970. *The New Deal and the Last Hurrah.* Pittsburgh: University of Pittsburgh Press.

Steinhoff, Patricia, and Milton Diamond. 1977. *Abortion Politics: The Hawaii Experience.* Honolulu: University Press of Hawaii.

Stone, Deborah A. 1989. "Causal Stories and the Formation of Policy Agendas." *Political Science Quarterly* 104 (2): 281–300.

Sumner, L. W. 1981. *Abortion and Moral Theory.* Princeton, N.J.: Princeton University Press.

Tarrow, Sidney. 1994. *Power in Movement: Social Movements, Collective Action, and Politics.* Cambridge: Cambridge University Press.

Tatalovich, Raymond, and Byron W. Daynes. 1981. *The Politics of Abortion: A Study of Community Conflict in Public Policymaking.* New York: Praeger.

Tilly, Charles. 1978. *From Mobilization to Revolution.* Reading, Mass.: Addison-Wesley.

Traina, Frank J. 1975. "Diocesan Mobilization Against Abortion Law Reform." Ph.D. dissertation, Cornell University.

United States Catholic Conference. 1967. *Annual Report,* pp. 40–43. Washington, D.C.: The Administrative Board.

———. 1968. *Annual Report,* p. 67. Washington, D.C.: The Administrative Board.

Vertaga, Pat, et al. 1972. "Abortion Cases in the United States." *Women's Rights Law Reporter* 1 (Spring): 50–55.

Walsh, Lawrence. 1972. "57% Back Abortions, Statewide Poll Says." *The Pittsburgh Press,* February 23, p. 43.

Weber, Michael. 1988. *Don't Call Me Boss: David L. Lawrence, Pittsburgh's Renaissance Mayor.* Pittsburgh: University of Pittsburgh Press.

Wertz, Richard W., and Dorothy C. Wertz. 1989. *Lying-In: A History of Childbirth in America.* New Haven: Yale University Press.

Westin, Alan F. 1967. *Privacy and Freedom.* New York: Atheneum.

Wetstein, Matthew W. 1996. *Abortion Rates in the United States: The Influence of Opinion and Policy.* New York: State University of New York Press.

Wharton, Linda J. 1991. "Gender and the Constitution: 200 years of Struggle for Women's Equality." Pp. 153–63 in *The Bill of Rights: A Bicentennial View,* edited by Mark I. Bernstein et al. A Project of the Pennsylvania Bar Association, Bill of Rights Bicentennial Commission. Baltimore: Gateway Press.

Williams, Glanville. 1957. *The Sanctity of Life and the Criminal Law.* New York: Knopf.

Wilson, James Q. 1962. *The Amateur Democrat: Club Politics in Three Cities.* Chicago: University of Chicago Press.

Women Concerned for the Unborn Child. 1972. *Newsletter* 1 (10 and 11). Pittsburgh, Pa.

———. 1974. *Newsletter* 2 (8). Pittsburgh, Pa.

Zelman, Patricia G. 1980. *Women, Work and National Policy: The Kennedy-Johnson Years.* Ann Arbor, Mich.: UMI Research.

Zyskowski, Bob. 1974. "Let Your Legislators Know How You Feel About Veto Override." *The Catholic Standard and Times* (Philadelphia, Pa.), September 5, p. 1.

Archives/Private Papers

Cisler, Lucinda (cofounder of New Yorkers for Abortion Law Repeal). Private papers. New York, N.Y.

Concern for Health Options: Information, Care, and Education (CHOICE). Files. Philadelphia, Pa.

Cusak, Dr. Ruth (chairwoman of the NOW Committee on Abortion Policy). Private papers. Miller Place, N.Y.

Family Planning Oral History Project Records. Schlesinger Library, Radcliffe Institute, Harvard University, Cambridge, Mass.

Ferson, Jean (president of Philadelphia NOW). Private papers. Philadelphia, Pa.

Greenwald, Pat (early member of the Clergy Consultation Service). Private papers. Harrisburg, Pa.

Lader, Lawrence. Papers. Rare Books and Manuscript Division, Astor, Lenox, and Tilden Foundation. New York Public Library. New York, N.Y.

Lange, Nancy (early member of the Committee for Progressive Legislation). Private papers. Schenectady, N.Y.

Pennsylvania Catholic Conference. Files. Harrisburg, Pa.

People Concerned for the Unborn Child. Files. Pittsburgh, Pa.

Schlesinger Library, Radcliffe Institute, Harvard University. Cambridge, Mass.

Smith, Ruth Proskauer (co-chair of the Committee for the Cook-Leichter Bill). Private papers. New York, N.Y.

Stengle, Sylvia (founder of Lehigh Valley Abortion Rights Association). Private papers. Bethlehem, Pa.

United States Catholic Conference Library. Washington, D.C. .

Urban Archive. Samuel Paley Library, Temple University. Philadelphia, Pa.

Weis, Sue (president, board of directors, Women's Health Services). Private papers. Dresher, Pa.

Index of Cases

189

General Index